INTEREST RATES AND ASSET PRICES

by the same author

THE ECONOMICS OF REAL PROPERTY

An analysis of property values
and patterns of use

INTEREST RATES
AND ASSET PRICES

BY

RALPH TURVEY
*Reader in Economics
in the
University of London*

LONDON
GEORGE ALLEN & UNWIN LTD
RUSKIN HOUSE   MUSEUM STREET

FIRST PUBLISHED IN 1960

© George Allen & Unwin Ltd., 1960

PRINTED IN GREAT BRITAIN
in 11 point Times Roman type
BY HAZELL WATSON AND VINEY LTD
AYLESBURY AND SLOUGH

TO SHEILA

PREFACE

MOST of this book was written while I was a Ford Foundation Visiting Research Professor at the University of Chicago in 1958–9. I am much indebted to the University for the opportunity which this appointment afforded and am extremely grateful to the members of the Department of Economics there for making my stay so enjoyable and stimulating. In particular I learnt a great deal from discussions in the Money and Banking Workshop, especially with James W. Ford, Milton Friedman, Reuben Kessel and David Meiselman. My colleagues at the London School of Economics have also contributed much helpful advice, notably David Knox, Kelvin Lancaster, A. W. H. Phillips and Maurice Peston. In addition, William Baumol, A. J. Hagger and Brian Tew made many useful suggestions. Lastly I am indebted to Ronald Conley, Fordyce A. Voss of the F.H.A. Division of Research and Statistics, R. Duane Saunders of the Treasury Department Debt Analysis Staff and Stephen Taylor of the Federal Reserve Board Flow of Funds Section for statistical assistance. The computations for Table V were carried out by Univac at the University of Chicago.

London School of Economics
March 1960

CONTENTS

I

INTRODUCTION

THIS book presents a statement of the theory of asset price formation. The aim is to set out a theory which meets three requirements; its relation to ordinary economic theory should be apparent, it should be simple and, finally, it should be directly relevant to the real world. More specifically, it should be based on the same sort of assumptions as other parts of economic theory; it should contain relatively few variables and it should be testable.

The analysis developed below is an aggregative version of a general theory, so this must first be sketched. This general static theory of asset prices—and thus of interest rates—is very simple. In fact it is so simple and so general that it is of hardly any use, as the reader can ascertain by looking at the elegant statement of it by Makower and Marschak in their article 'Assets, Prices and Monetary Theory'.[1] Like all general equilibrium theory, the general static theory of asset prices is difficult to expound and it will suffice here to put the matter baldly. The essential thing is that given (*a*) the initial distribution of assets[2] and (*b*) the asset preferences of each owner of wealth, there will be an equilibrium pattern of asset holdings and of asset prices. In general we would suppose that the price of any one asset will be relatively higher, *ceteris paribus*, the less

---

[1] *Economica* 1938, reprinted in *Readings in Price Theory*.

[2] It is the distribution of assets as a whole between different owners, not of each particular asset which matters, but this cannot be expressed by assuming the initial distribution of wealth to be given since wealth cannot be measured until prices are determined.

there is of it, the more popular it is and the more wealth is concentrated in the hands of people who value it particularly highly.

These propositions are no doubt acceptable to most economists. If the special cases which produce occasional rather recherché exceptions are ignored, they require two major assumptions about the nature of asset demand. The first of these is that if wealth increases, given constant relative asset prices, the demand for all assets will increase. The second assumption is that given total wealth, a fall in the relative price of any one asset will increase the demand for it.

Let us adopt the assumptions, and start by supposing that all assets are superior with respect to wealth and that all assets are substitutes for money (though not necessarily for all other assets as well). Now a rise in the price of any asset relatively to the price of money implies a rise in the money price of the asset; the price of money cannot fall because it is always unity. This enables us to go a little beyond the general propositions mentioned above. *Ceteris paribus* any of the following differences in the given elements of the situation will make the equilibrium price of asset X higher in absolute money terms:

(1) a reduction in the quantity of X;
(2) an increased desire to hold X;
(3) a greater initial holding of assets (or smaller holding of debts) by people whose desire to hold X is particularly strong;
(4) an increase in the quantity of money;
(5) a decreased desire to hold money, for example in consequence of a reduction in the aggregate value of transactions.

Now this theory, although not trivial, is not very useful as it stands. It is too general. What is needed, therefore, is

14

a more down to earth analysis in terms of the actual assets existing in the economy as we know it. This in turn requires that the analysis be made highly aggregative, for only thus can it be expressed in a comprehensible manner. If the degree of aggregation were low there would be too many variables to handle.

The purpose of this book is to present the theory usefully and simply. The following pages, in other words, contain a restatement of asset price theory which is a simple aggregative version of the general theory just sketched out.

Before the plan of the book is outlined in detail there are some general remarks to be made. Firstly, the reader will not find any account of the 'ultimate' determinants of asset prices and interest rates. The reason is that the analysis is a partial one, i.e. it is concerned with one part of the economy only, namely the asset market. Thus while the impact upon asset prices of happenings in the rest of the economy enters into the analysis, nothing is said about the effect of asset prices upon the rest of the economy. The theory provides only one part of a macro model in the same way as, say, a book on the consumption function. In order to answer questions about the effect on the equilibrium level of interest rates of changes in the economy this theory and a theory of consumption would both be necessary, but neither the one nor the other would be sufficient.

A second general remark is that the bulk of the following discussion relates to prices and interest rates on Government securities. This might be criticized on the grounds that it restricts the applicability of the theory to economies where there is a sizeable national debt. It might be added that even in such economies it would be more useful and interesting to analyse the prices of other assets, real assets, for instance, or shares. Both these points have merit, but nonetheless there are very good grounds for the course followed. As is explained in

Chapter IV the theory applies to real assets just as much as to the national debt. Attention is centred on the latter, however, because while there are hardly any data on the volume and price level of real assets there are plenty of statistics of the national debt. Since one of the aims of the book is to formulate a theory in terms of observable variables, a theory, that is to say, which is testable, it is necessary to concentrate on the national debt. Chapter VI shows how the theory can be applied to explain yields on the U.S. national debt in the post-war period; to do the same for real assets is simply impossible owing to the lack of data.

There remains the point that it may be more useful to explain yields on private debt and shares than on the national debt. It will be shown, however, that this is more complicated so that as a first step it is justifiable to concentrate on the simpler analysis of the level of yields on the national debt.

The last general remark to be made is that there is no mention of the relation between the loanable funds theory of interest and the liquidity preference theory, indeed the loanable funds approach is not mentioned at all. Since the topic of the consistency and relative merits of these two approaches is still a perennial subject for articles in the journals, this may occasion some surprise. My excuse is that I am only interested in theories which are testable and I do not know of any attempt to use or test the loanable funds theory. There have been many empirical discussions of liquidity preference theory, however, and this fact alone seems to me to make it the more interesting of the two approaches.

It will perhaps help the reader if the course of the following chapters is briefly described. The main argument runs through Chapters II, IV and VI. The first of these outlines the theory for the simplest case conceivable where there

16

are only two assets in the world, money and bonds, and only one asset-owning sector. This theory turns out to be the same as the liquidity preference theory with the stock of bonds brought in explicitly as an independent variable. Chapter IV then brings national income into the analysis and adds the stock of real assets as a third type of asset. The determination of the level of prices of real assets as well as that of bonds is discussed. Finally, in Chapter VI, the way in which the theory must be developed so as to make it directly applicable to the particular circumstances of a particular economy is illustrated. The example chosen is the United States during the post-war period, and the average yield on private non-bank holdings of the public debt constitutes the variable which is to be explained. Some statistical results are presented, not to provide quantitative evidence concerning the value of the parameters, which would require a more extensive and sophisticated analysis, but rather to show that the theory is indeed testable.

The other chapters take up some particular issues. Chapter III is concerned with the transactions demand for money. Chapter V deals with a possible objection to the theory, namely that it misses out the stock of private debt from the determinants of asset prices. It is shown that this involves no logical difficulty, though this is not to deny the empirical possibility that behaviour relationships may in some cases prove to be more stable in a less aggregative model. Chapter VII takes up a related topic, discussing the nature of financial intermediaries. This is rather by the way of an excursion, but the topic has been a popular one of late and the existence of financial intermediaries affects the level of interest rates.

Chapter VIII contains an extension of the theory to the determination of the relation between long and short term interest rates. Finally, Chapter IX sketches the way in which the theory might be developed to deal with two other topics: the determination of the money supply and the determination of share prices.

It remains to say something about the intellectual antecedents of this book. It started as an article 'Consistency and Consolidation in the Theory of Interest' published in *Economica* in 1954 and now largely incorporated in Chapter II. The basic idea, that asset prices depend upon relative asset qualities, is of course too obvious to be attributable to any particular author, but its application to aggregative interest theory is far from being a commonplace. Three works in particular which made this application led me to attempt to restate interest theory in such a way that consistency was achieved and the analysis centred round wealth owners' choice of assets.

The first of these was Professor Metzler's well-known article 'Wealth, Saving and the Rate of Interest'[1]; the second was Mrs Robinson's 'The Rate of Interest'[2], and the third was A. M. Khusro's 'An Investigation of Liquidity Preference'.[3] This paper seems to me to be one of the best empirical studies yet published and deserves to be much more widely known. This does not exhaust the list of authors whose work is relevant; no doubt I have absorbed ideas from dozens of others, both directly and indirectly.

[1] *Journal of Political Economy*, April 1951.
[2] In her book of that title.
[3] *Yorkshire Bulletin of Economic and Social Research*, January 1952.

18

II

BOND PREFERENCE AND
LIQUIDITY PREFERENCE

IN the previous chapter five *ceteris paribus* propositions derived from the general static theory of asset prices were enunciated. The fourth and fifth of these stated that the price of asset X would be raised by an increase in the quantity of money or by a decreased desire to hold money. If X is a paper asset yielding fixed periodic interest payments, and if the desire to hold money is assumed to rise if the level of national money income increases, these two propositions can be stated another way. The rate of interest, we can say, is a function of the quantity of money and the national income.

Now this is nothing but the liquidity preference theory of interest expressed as briefly as is possible. The advantage of this way of arriving at the theory is that the importance and relevance of certain questions are immediately relevant. Firstly, the liquidity preference theory as usually stated contains no reference to the first three of the five propositions. Should it not do so? Secondly, expositions of the theory customarily refer to 'the' rate of interest as though there were only one rate. Can it not explain the prices of several assets, and not only the price of those yielding a fixed income?

The following analysis deals with these questions. The method followed is to set out a theoretical approach which is both an aggregative version of the general theory with its myriad of assets and of wealth owners and a generalization and extension of the liquidity preference theory.[1] In this chapter the simplest possible case is examined, where there is only one paper asset other than money and where all owners of this asset are aggregated into a single group. This means that the economy is divided into only two sectors, the asset owning group which we call the private sector and the sector whose liability these paper assets are, the monetary sector (the banking system and the Government). Let the single asset be called bonds. Then the wealth accounts—interlocking balance sheets—of the economy take the simple form shown in Table I, where L and A stand for liability and asset respectively. This potted description of the monetary system makes it clear that there are only two sectors and only two assets and that the set-up is as simple as it is possible to imagine.

TABLE I

Asset	Sector	
	Monetary	Private
Money	L	A
Bonds	L	A

Each of the two columns in the table constitutes a consolidated balance sheet for the sector as a whole. Money and bonds are the only intersector assets and liabilities;

[1] The following pages draw upon my paper 'Consistency and Consolidation in the Theory of Interest', *Economica*, November 1954. A similar model is presented by Brechling in 'A Note on Bondholding and the Liquidity Preference Theory of Interest', *Review of Economic Studies*, Vol. XXIV, 3.

purely intrasector assets and liabilities, if any, cancel out and are not shown since the table records only the net position of each sector with respect to each asset and liability. As the table is written, therefore, real assets do not exist and the only items in the balance sheets are paper assets and liabilities. This lacuna will be filled in Chapter IV. Meanwhile it may be supposed that such real assets as exist are non-negotiable, permanent and non-augmentable so that they have no prices and can neither be used up nor acquired. Their presence can therefore exert no influence save indirectly, by affecting preferences as between money and bonds. Similarly the role of money income, the price level and hence real income too will be totally neglected in this chapter by supposing them all to be given and constant. Real assets and income will be introduced into the analysis in the following chapter.

Let us take the quantity of money and the number of bonds as given, at M and N respectively. It is convenient to measure the number of bonds in terms of the income to which they constitute a claim, so that one bond is a claim to one pound per annum. The price of a bond is then the reciprocal of the rate of interest on bonds. If we denote this price by H, then the wealth of the private sector is:

$$W = M + NH$$

The assumptions of the general theory of asset prices discussed in Chapter I were that all assets are superior with respect to wealth and that they are all substitutes for one another. Particularizing these assumptions for the present case, we may suppose that *ceteris paribus* the stock of bonds demanded by the private sector will be increased by a rise in wealth, W, or by a rise in their interest rate, that is a fall in their price, H. It is, however, convenient to write the demand equation for bonds in terms of the value of bonds demanded, D_N, rather than the number. Assuming linearity and neglecting constant terms in order to keep the algebra simple, we therefore have

$$D_N = cW + dH$$

Since both money and bonds are superior, a rise in wealth will raise the demand for both, so that the demand for bonds will increase but by a smaller amount than wealth. c is therefore positive but less than unity. d, on the other hand, may be either positive or negative. If, for instance, the number of bonds demanded is inelastic with respect to price, d will be positive.

Equilibrium requires that the demand of the private sector for bonds equals the supply, i.e.

$$D_N = NH$$

There is no need to write out the demand equation for money since this equals wealth less the demand for bonds. We therefore have three equations which can be solved for H to give

$$H = \frac{cM}{(1 - c)\,N - d}$$

It is clear that the five propositions of the general theory concerning the price of asset X which were set out in Chapter I apply here. H will rise if:

(1) the number of bonds falls (N falls);
(2), (3) and (5) the desire to hold bonds rises. Since money is the only alternative asset, this comes to the same thing as a reduced desire to hold money (c increases);
(4) the quantity of money is increased (M rises).

The solution for H contains three variables: H, M and N. If we wish to examine the relationship between only two out of the three, some *ceteris paribus* assumption must be made in order to deal with the third variable. From all the various possible relationships four may be picked out here; they are the relationships between

(1) H and N, with M constant;
(2) H and N, when N is changed through open market operations, so that M and N change in opposite directions;
(3) H and M, with N constant;
(4) H and M, when M is changed through open market operations, so that N and M change in opposite directions.

The first two of these concentrate attention upon bonds, while the second two concentrate attention upon the quantity of money. Thus although all four relationships are merely different two-dimensional derivations from the fundamental three-dimensional relationship between the three variables, there is a difference in emphasis so that the first pair of relationships can be said to express a bond preference theory of bond price, and the second pair to express a liquidity preference theory of bond price.

With a simple monetary system of the sort described in Table I the bond preference theory and the liquidity preference theory are thus equivalent to one another. Since the second is the usual one, let us continue the discussion in terms of liquidity preference and in order to make things even more familiar let us speak of the rate of interest on bonds rather than of their price. We now wish to compare the relationships between the rate of interest and the quantity of money given N or, alternatively, as the quantity of money is altered through the sale or purchase of bonds by the monetary sector. In Diagram I the continuous curves show the first of these relationships; thus the curve N=a shows how the rate of interest varies as the quantity of money alters when the number of bonds is constant and equal to a. These curves thus each present one cross section of the surface showing the relationship between the rate of interest, the number of bonds and the quantity of money; they may therefore be called 'constant number of bonds liquidity preference curves'. They slope downwards because an increase in the quantity of money constitutes an increase in wealth and this means a greater demand for bonds. The higher demand for bonds means in turn a lower yield (higher price) which contributes an additional increase in wealth.

The dotted curve in Diagram I shows another kind of liquidity preference curve. Here an increase in the quantity of money is accompanied by a decrease in the number of bonds, and vice versa, as when open market operations take place. For instance, starting from point E the monetary sector increases the quantity of money by CD by purchasing b—a bonds.[1] Thus curves such as EF may be called 'open market operations liquidity preference curves'. It is clear that they must be steeper than the constant number of bonds curves. If, for instance, the quantity of money increases by CD, the rate of interest will fall by GF more if b—a bonds are bought than if the number of bonds remains unchanged at b. This follows from the fact that, other things remaining the same, a fall in the number of bonds will lower the rate of interest (i.e. raise the price of bonds).

It is clear that if an exposition of liquidity (or bond) preference theory is to be adequate there must be an explicit statement of which kind of curve is being employed. One or other of the two kinds mentioned seems to be what most writers on liquidity preference have had in mind, but

[1] A difficulty in the construction of these curves deserves mention. Two purchases of £x worth of bonds may acquire more bonds than one purchase of £2x, while two sales each of which realizes £x may dispose of fewer bonds than one sale which realizes £2x. Kragh has discussed this point in 'The Meaning and use of Liquidity curves in Keynesian interest theory', *International Economic Papers*, No. 5, p. 161.

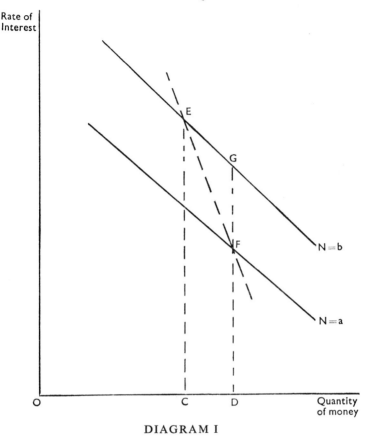

DIAGRAM I

other kinds could be constructed, for instance a 'constant wealth liquidity preference curve'. It is important to note that there is not just one curve of each type, but an infinite number of each. It follows that theoretical discussions which are couched in terms of one single liquidity preference curve logically imply some particular assumption such as that the number of bonds is fixed at some par-

25

ticular level, that the number of bonds and the quantity of money can change from given initial amounts only through the medium of bond dealings by the monetary sector or that wealth is constant at some given level.

To sum up, what has been done in this chapter is to set out the most highly aggregated case of the general theory of asset prices, the case of only two sectors and only two assets. I have shown that this can be expressed either as the liquidity preference theory or as the bond preference theory and that whichever alternative is followed there is not one but a multiplicity of curves to be dealt with. The number of bonds is just as important as the quantity of money and should therefore enter into the analysis explicitly.

III

THE TRANSACTIONS MOTIVE
FOR HOLDING MONEY

THE demand for money as a way of holding wealth partly arises because wealth owners sometimes expect asset prices to fall and partly because they abhor the capital uncertainty involved in holding some assets. Quite apart from this, however, money is also held in order to be spent by firms and households which expect to make payments in excess of receipts in the near future. In Keynesian terms there is not only a speculative and a precautionary motive; there is also a transactions motive for holding money.

It is generally accepted that the strength of the transactions motive rises with the total value of transactions and that this in turn is an increasing function of the level of income. These propositions will be accepted in the following chapters, but by way of a digression this chapter first examines some complications which deserve more attention than they are generally given. The following analysis starts with an artificially simple case and then relaxes the restrictive assumptions.

As a first step, consider the money requirements of a single household (or firm) which has a definite schedule of payments to make and receipts to accept in the near future. The schedule is definite in the sense that there is no uncertainty and the household has no discretion concerning either the amount or the timing of payments and receipts. It is assumed that these payments and receipts

27

form a regular repetitive cycle and that total payments and receipts over the cycle equal one another.

Under these conditions, which rule out any choice on the part of the household, the concept of a transactions balance can be precisely defined. The household's money holding at any point of time will equal its initial money holding plus all receipts accepted up to then, minus all payments made up to then. If the smallest amount held is, say, £70 on March 15th, then the household's transactions holding at any point of time equals its total money holding at that point of time minus £70. Its transactions balance is thus defined as the minimum amount of money which the household must own in order to avoid default on the payments it has to make. Thus, if the household were robbed of its £70 on March 15th, it could nevertheless meet all its obligations, so that its transactions balance on, say, March 16th is its actual holding on that day less £70.

Note two features of the transactions balance so defined. First, it can never be negative, except for banks and Governments which create money, but will be zero on March 15th and positive at most other points of time. (It is true that one speaks of a household owing money, but this means that it has a negative holding of I.O.U.'s, not a negative holding of money.) Secondly, it will fluctuate from day to day except when payments and receipts are equal in any one day.

The time pattern of the household's transaction holding of money will be altered by any change in the pattern of payments and receipts except when they change equally, simultaneously and in the same direction. Such equi-proportional changes may not happen in practice, but they are important in theoretical discussions. In static general equilibrium analysis it is often argued that a change in the quantity of money will change all prices proportionately, leaving all real quantities unaffected. But any other sort of change in payments and receipts will alter the time pattern of transactions balances. For instance the mere postponement of a payment from Tuesday to Friday will raise the transactions holding during the intervening period (without lowering it at other times) unless the minimum point previously fell in that period and no longer does. In this latter case the postponement of the payment may lower transactions holdings before Tuesday and after Friday by shifting the minimum point to, say, Saturday and raising it. Thus, to put the matter paradoxically, the timing of a change in timing determines whether and when transactions holdings are increased or decreased.

It follows that no general proposition can be made about the effects of a change in the frequency of payments or receipts. An employee, for instance, who shifts over from weekly receipts of wages to monthly receipt will have a larger transactions balance on average if his spending is spread evenly over the month but a smaller average balance if his spending is heavily concentrated at the beginning of the month.[1] On the other hand it is clear that if all receipts and all payments change equi-proportionately, so that there is a change in the scale of transactions without any change in timing, the transactions balance at all points of time will change by the same proportion.

An alteration in the level of a household's (or firm's) transactions will, however, rarely take the form of an equal proportionate change in all its receipts and payments. If, for instance, a man receives an x per cent salary increase he is most unlikely to increase all his expenditures by x per cent. Thus the change in his total receipts and payments per unit period will be associated with a change

[1] For a numerical example of a case where an increased frequency of payment by A to B raises the transactions balances of both parties, see my paper 'On the Transactions Demand for Money' in *25 Economic Essays in Honor of Erik Lindahl*. The present chapter is partly based on this paper.

in the timing structure of that total. Now any actual change can be split into two components, the first of which is the change in the timing of receipts and payments from the old to the new structure, with a constant total, the second component being an equi-proportionate change in all receipts and payments from the old level to the new level. These might be called the timing component and the scale component respectively.

The argument above was that it is not possible to say anything *a priori* about the effect on the household's transactions holding of the time component. On the other hand the effect of the scale component is clear. The joint effect of the two components can therefore be in either direction. Yet in a probabilistic sense the joint effect is equal to the scale effect since the average transactions balance at any point of time of all possible time schedules of payments and receipts will rise proportionately with scale.

The analysis of this purely mechanistic case where there is a definite cycle of payments and receipts thus provides two conclusions. The first is that nothing can be said *a priori* about the effect of changes in timing. In particular it is not true that an increased frequency of one or more particular payments or receipts will generally lower transactions balances. The second conclusion is that transactions balances will move in proportion with total transactions only in a probability sense.

It has been shown that the transactions balance of a household or firm will fluctuate over time. Since the payment which reduces one person's money holding necessarily constitutes the receipt which raises somebody else's holding of money, the same is not true of the aggregate of transactions balances. This aggregate will therefore not reflect the periodical fluctuations of individual transactions holdings, save possibly to a trifling extent as a result of delay between the payment and receipt of money. The remarks made above otherwise apply in their entirety, so that proportionality between aggregate transactions and aggregate transactions balances can be alleged only as probable, even under the assumptions made above that each person and firm has a known and certain schedule of payments and receipts to which he must conform.

The next step is to remove these assumptions. If a person has a large excess of payments over receipts due sometime in the future he may, as assumed above, hold sufficient money over the intervening period to meet that excess. There are other possibilities open to him, however. Firstly, he may postpone the payments or hasten the receipts by altering the timing of some transactions. For instance he may decide to put off buying a car, doing without its services for a while. Secondly, he might lend out money on short term, obtaining repayment when his large payments fall due. For instance a firm may put money on deposit account or buy treasury bills. This involves some cost and bother but earns interest. Thirdly (the list is not meant to be exhaustive) there is the possibility of spending any money not required immediately and then borrowing later when the heavy payments become due, for example by obtaining a bank loan or issuing finance paper.

It is interesting to note that the second and third alternatives both may involve additional financial transactions. In other words by increasing both payments and receipts an economy of transactions balances is achieved. The point made above that some increases in the level of transactions will actually lower transactions balances is thus reaffirmed.

A general and formal analysis of optimal behaviour in respect of these and other alternatives would be excessively complicated. Professors Baumol and Tobin have constructed simple models, both assuming that lending at a

31

single interest rate constitutes the only alternative to holding money.[1] Their conclusions appear to have more general validity, however, and can be explained intuitively without any formal apparatus as follows.

If there were no cost and bother of borrowing or lending, that is if both the money cost of fees and charges and the trouble involved by the necessary paper work and negotiation were zero, it would always be worth while to undertake money-economizing transactions and nobody would hold any money. But they are positive, which explains why people hold money. These costs are partly independent of the absolute size of the transactions so that though they will presumably rise with the amount of money being borrowed or lent they will do so by a much smaller proportion. On the other hand the interest paid or earned will normally rise by the same proportion. Hence the difference between them, which is the net cost of borrowing and the net gain from lending, will rise by a larger proportion. It follows that any change in transactions which, in the absence of short-term lending or borrowing designed to economize money holdings, would raise transactions balances will make it more profitable than before to borrow or lend. Consequently the amount of transactions of this sort will increase. Thus in the case of an equi-proportional increase in all other payments and receipts, the amount of money held by some households and firms will rise less than proportionately and the amount of such money-economizing financial transactions will rise more than proportionately. In the case of an increase in other payments and receipts which involves a change in timing, these conclusions of course hold only as probabilities.

---

[1] William J. Baumol, 'The Transactions Demand for Cash: An Inventory Theoretic Approach', *Quarterly Journal of Economics*, November 1952; James Tobin, 'The Interest Elasticity of Transactions Demand for Cash', *Review of Economics and Statistics*, August 1956.

These two conclusions be it noted, assume that the schedule of the cost and bother of undertaking money-economizing transactions remains unchanged.

Given the level and timing of non-money-economizing transaction, the transactions demand for money and the amount of money-economizing transactions will depend upon the net gain to be had from this latter kind of transaction. The direction of this influence can be deduced from what has been said above: other things equal there will be more such transactions the smaller is the cost and bother which they involve, the higher are the interest rates obtainable by lenders and the cheaper and more available is credit to borrowers. The relevance of both borrowing and of lending rates of interest means that a general change in the level of interest rates has a double effect. Consider a fall, for example. On the one hand the gain to be had from lending temporarily surplus funds is reduced, which by itself would tend to raise the transactions demand for money. On the other hand, the need to carry money to meet a future excess of payments over receipts is reduced by the greater facility and cheapness with which funds can be acquired when the time comes. This factor by itself would therefore work in the opposite direction to the fall in lending rates, tending to lower transactions demand.[1] The net effect of a general change in interest rates may therefore be in either direction. On the present abstract level of analysis it is thus impossible to say how the transactions demand for money will respond to short-term interest rates.

This conclusion may seem paradoxical. It must be remembered, however, that it relates only to the effect of

[1] Richard T. Selden expresses the point in terms of money substitutes and money complements. See pp. 209–10 of his paper 'Monetary Velocity in the United States' in *Studies in the Quantity Theory of Money*, ed. Friedman.

interest rates upon money-economizing transactions and hence upon transactions demand all other things remaining the same. There is no contradiction involved in stating that a rise in transactions demand, *ceteris paribus*, will raise interest rates.

The assumption that the amount and timing of non-money economizing transactions is known with certainty must now be abandoned. The point that many firms and households may be sent bills unexpectedly or accept receipts which were not anticipated requires no exemplification. It is clear too that the larger the amount of money held and the greater the availability of credit the less will be the likelihood of financial embarrassment. The possession of money in excess of that required to meet any excess of foreseen payments over foreseen receipts therefore confers security upon its holder. The more he holds, the smaller is the chance of unforeseen transactions forcing him to make inconvenient and perhaps expensive changes in his plans. On the other hand, the cheaper and more readily available is credit if required to meet such contingencies, the smaller is the need to provide for them by holding money. Thus while a rise in lending rates of interest increases the (opportunity) cost of holding money, and will therefore turn the balance of advantage towards some reduction in money holding, a rise in borrowing rates will have the opposite effect. The conclusion reached above thus applies when uncertainty is present. The only difference is that long-term as well as short-term lending rates of interest are relevant, since it is now a question of persons and firms reducing their money holdings over long periods as well as for short periods.

Just as interest rates have more than one effect on the transactions demand for money, so does national money income, though here the different effects will normally work in the same direction. In so far as a rise in money national income involves an increase in the total of non-money-economizing transactions it will probably raise the transactions demand for money, though less than proportionately to these transactions, increasing money-economizing transactions more than proportionately to them. This merely repeats what has been said above. If the cost of making money-economizing transactions rises at the same time, the point about proportions does not apply. In all cases, however, the statement concerning the transactions effect is only a probability statement.

The question of the extent to which money national income and total non-money-economizing transactions move together is an empirical one. The part of national income consisting of imputed items and business saving does not involve any money payment. On the other hand there are many non-money-economizing transactions which are not income payments. The main types of such transactions are the purchase of final goods and services, taxes and transfers, the purchase of intermediate goods and services and the turnover of assets. Hence starting with national income it is necessary to carry out the following additions and subtractions (indicated by plus and minus signs) to get to total non-money-economizing transactions:

— imputed income and gross business saving;
+ gross national expenditure net of imputed items;
+ taxes and transfers;
+ purchases of intermediate goods and services;
+ payments for paper assets and existing real assets.

This is a rough approximation which only indicates the major kinds of transaction other than the payment of income, but it suffices for the present purpose. Note that the last item includes not only all lending and borrowing but also all the shuffling round of assets except money-economizing transactions.

35

One would suppose that the first four items change in relation to income only slowly, as the structure of the economy alters, while the last item may be more volatile. Some evidence relating to the U.S. is presented in Diagram II[1] where the horizontal axis measures (approximately) gross national income net of imputed items while the vertical axis measures total transactions other than payments for paper assets and existing real assets. This scatter, shown by dots, covering the years 1939–56 inclusive, indicates that both rose together during the period ($r = \cdot99$) with a structural change in the years 1944–6. The vertical axis also shows a series of bank debits which presumably provides an indicator of movements in the total of all transactions. The scatter for the years 1943–56 is shown by crosses and displays much the same pattern in relation to gross national income ($r = \cdot96$) with a structural change after the war (and possibly in 1953–4).

All this relates to one of two effects upon the transactions demand of a rise in national money income. A second effect arises in so far as this change involves a rise in real income *per capita*. If households become better off they will demand more security from financial embarrassment and so hold larger amounts of money (in real terms) to provide against uncertainty concerning their payments and receipts.[2] Putting the point another way, a falling marginal utility of income will lead people to sacrifice more income

[1] *Sources:* Debits to demand deposits except interbank and Government deposits, *Federal Reserve Bulletin*; non-financial uses of funds and the G.N.P. identifiable therein, *Flow of Funds in the United States 1939–53* and the *Federal Reserve Bulletin*, April and October 1957. All figures are annual totals in billions of dollars. Comparable figures for earlier years are not available.

[2] Professor Friedman's researches lead him to maintain that, at least so far as secular movements are concerned, real 'permanent' income is the major determinant of the (real) demand for money. See his paper in the *Journal of Political Economy*, August 1959: 'The demand for money—some theoretical and empirical results'.

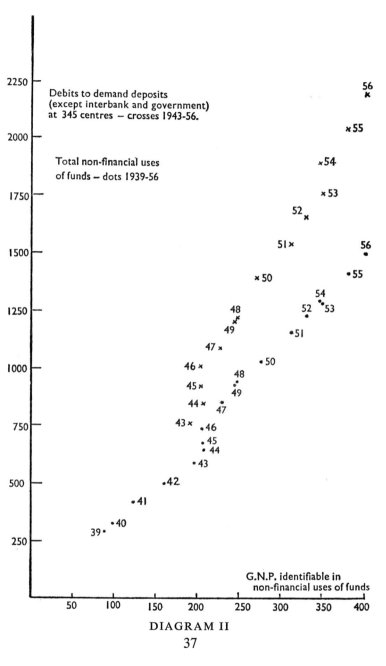

Debits to demand deposits (except interbank and government) at 345 centres — crosses 1943-56.

Total non-financial uses of funds — dots 1939-56

G.N.P. identifiable in non-financial uses of funds

DIAGRAM II

37

for convenience and safety. Thus like the transactions effect, the income effect is positive and the two effects will work in the same direction unless non-money-economizing transactions move in the opposite direction to real income *per capita*. Other things being equal, the larger the rise in real income associated with a given rise in money income, the larger will be the resulting increase in the demand for money.

Under the mechanistic assumptions made at the beginning of this chapter, it was possible to speak not only of the transactions motive for holding money but also of the amount of money held because of this motive, i.e. of transactions balances. This is no longer the case, however, once choice and uncertainty are introduced, for then, as has been shown, interest rates and income become determinants of transactions demand. Interest rates, and perhaps income too, also affect the non-transactions demand for money, however, which makes it impossible to split the determinants of the total demand for money into two completely different groups. Consequently this demand cannot be regarded as the sum of a transactions demand determined by one set of forces and a non-transactions demand determined by a different set. A person's holding of money cannot therefore be divided, even conceptually, into two parts except on a purely *ex post* basis, and this is of no great interest in the present discussion.

It is of course still possible to discuss the effect upon a person's or firm's total demand for money of a *ceteris paribus* change in the pattern of transactions—e.g. of a rise in a household's monthly income receipt and consequent changes in its expenditures. The point to be noted here, however, is that the magnitude of this effect may partly depend upon the level of some of the factors impounded in *ceteris paribus*, factors relevant to the non-transactions motive as well as to the transactions motive.

Transactions balances can therefore only be measured in the case of money holders who are known to have no other motive for holding money, if there be such. Except in this case the propositions concerning the transactions motive for holding money can only be tested as part of an analysis of the total demand for money. Propositions about aggregate transactions balances are therefore useful only as a convenient shorthand when the factors relevant to the strength of the transactions motive are under discussion.

This last statement is one conclusion reached in this chapter. Another is that it is only a probability that the strength of the transactions motive for holding money varies in the same direction as national income since a change in the frequency of payments may either raise or lower demand and since transactions in paper assets and existing real assets may vary independently of income. If the total value of transactions does vary proportionately with national income, the extent to which changes in income are real changes or merely price-level changes affects their impact upon the strength of the transactions motive in two ways. On the one hand, a rise in money income will raise the demand for money by a larger extent the smaller is the rise in the price level, for then the stronger will be the real income effect. On the other hand, a small rise in the price level will presumably involve a small increase in the cost and bother of transactions so that money-economizing transactions will be engaged in to a much greater extent and the demand for money will rise relatively little. Which of these two effects is stronger is difficult to say. Lastly, it has been shown that interest rates affect transactions demand, though *a priori* it is not clear in which direction this effect is exerted.

IV

THE INFLUENCE OF INCOME AND
OF REAL ASSETS

THE theory expounded in Chapter II related to an exceedingly simple state of affairs. It is the purpose of this chapter to advance the analysis by bringing in two additional factors which are too important to ignore. One of these, discussed in the previous chapter, is that the demand for money depends partly upon the level of national income. The other is that reproducible and non-reproducible assets, such as farms, factories and houses, are negotiable and have prices. These real assets are alternatives to paper assets as ways of holding wealth, so that the yields that both offer are closely interconnected and the quantity of real assets is as relevant to the price of bonds as are the quantities of paper assets.

Let us therefore examine asset price formation in the system described in Table II which differs from Table I only by the inclusion of real assets as a third form in which the private sector can hold its wealth.

TABLE II

Asset	Sector	
	Monetary	Private
Money	L	A
Bonds	L	A
Real Assets	—	A

As before, let M represent the quantity of money and NH the number of bonds (each bond being a claim to £1 per annum) multiplied by the price of bonds. Let R be the income deriving from the ownership of real assets and Q the value of a right to £1 per annum of such income, then RQ is the total value of real assets and the wealth of the private sector is

$$W = M + NH + RQ$$

H and Q are thus capitalization factors, i.e. numbers of years purchase, and the quantities of bonds and real assets are measured in terms of the incomes derived from their ownership.

Let us suppose that the demand for money is an increasing function of wealth, W, and of money national income, Y.[1] (Since real income is also relevant, as explained in Chapter III, we must assume a given relationship between the price level and money income.) Assume further that, other things being equal, a fall in the yield of bonds or of real assets (i.e. a rise in H or in Q) will raise the demand for money. This substitutability assumption means that given total wealth and given the strength of the transactions motive for holding money, a fall in the yield of either of the other two assets will cause some shift into money from the asset whose yield has fallen. The demand

---

[1] Friedman, op. cit., suggests on p. 349 that his results can be interpreted in terms of an asset motive for holding money and that 'as permanent income rises, the total value of non-human wealth rises more rapidly than permanent income'. But even if it does not, his results would still be consistent with the above formulation if the wealth elasticity of the demand for money exceeds unity. The ratio of currency, demand and time deposits held by the private sector to its net worth showed an upward trend in the U.S. between 1896 and 1940 so far as one can judge by using Goldsmith's figures of national wealth from *A Study of Savings* Table W.1 in conjunction with some monetary time series collected by Friedman and Schwartz (as yet unpublished). The trend was not smooth, but any attempt to examine year to year fluctuations seems of dubious value in view of the uncertainty surrounding the current value wealth estimates.

for money, D_M, is therefore, assuming linearity and neglecting any constant term:

$$D_M = aW + bH + kQ + jY$$

All these constants are positive. a gives the effect upon the demand for money of changes in wealth. b and k indicate that the demand for money will be increased by a rise in H and Q, i.e. by a fall in the yield on bonds and real assets. Finally, f is also positive, indicating that the demand for money rises with national income.

The demand for bonds may be written similarly. Suppose that *ceteris paribus* the demand is increased by a rise in wealth, a fall in the yield of real assets (a rise in Q) or by a fall in income. The reason why income enters the demand equation is that if a fall in income lowers the demand for money it must raise the demand for some other asset. Let us again write the demand for bonds not as the number of bonds demanded, but as the value of bonds demanded:

$$D_N = cW + dH + eQ + fY$$

It follows from what has been said that c and e are positive and f is negative, while d may be either negative or positive.

There is no need to write out a demand equation for real assets, since this is given residually as the difference between wealth and the sum of the demands for bonds and real assets. Given equality between the demand and supply of money and of bonds, i.e.

$$D_M = M \text{ and } D_N = NH$$

the equations can be solved to give:

$$H = \frac{M[(1-a)(cR+e)+c(aR+k)] - Y[j(cR+e)+f(aR+k)]}{(N-cN-d)(aR+k)+(aN+b)(cR+b)}$$

The five propositions enunciated in Chapter I apply perfectly well to the present case. *Ceteris paribus* the price of bonds, H, will be raised by:

(1) a fall in the quantity of bonds (a reduction in N);
(2) and (3) an increased desire to hold bonds at the expense of both money and real assets (e.g. a rise in c and a smaller fall in a);[1]
(4) an increase in the quantity of money (a rise in M);
(5) a downward shift in the demand for money (e.g. a fall in a).

These results differ from those set out in Chapter II only by the addition of Y and R as additional items to be held constant. The arguments of that chapter therefore continue to hold for any given values of Y and of R and no restatement is necessary.

It would appear, however, that an additional proposition can be enunciated: that *ceteris paribus* a rise in the strength of the transactions demand for money will lower the price of bonds. This is correct but not very interesting. The reason is that the major determinant of transactions demand, total money income Y, and the money income from real assets, R, will normally move together. R, after all, is a component of Y. In a cyclical upswing, for example, the strength of the transactions motive for holding money will increase. This, taken by itself, would tend to lower the price of bonds. On the other hand, the income from real assets will also rise, and this factor, taken by

[1] If the increased desire to hold bonds were entirely, or almost entirely at the expense of real assets so that a did not fall there is a possibility that the price of bonds would fall rather than rise. An intuitive explanation of this case is as follows: Initially H will rise and Q will fall which would raise the demand for money (if b is large in relation to k). The attempt of wealth owners to acquire more money by selling more real assets may then so lower their price that the increase in their yield and a fall in wealth reduce the demand for bonds below its original level. Note that even if this happens, the price of bonds will have risen relatively to Q though lower in money terms.

itself, might either raise or lower the price of bonds. The net effect of the two changes taken together may therefore either be to lower or to raise the price of bonds.

The reason for this two-way possibility is as follows. A rise in income, by raising the demand for money, will cause a shift out of real assets which will lower Q. Q will also be lowered by an increase in R, the income from real assets. This fall in Q and the increased demand for money will cause a substitution into real assets and money respectively from bonds. These are the factors which tend to lower the price of bonds. On the other hand if the rise in R is large relatively to the fall in Q, RQ, the total value of real assets may rise. If so there will be some increase in the demand for bonds, since the rise in RQ constitutes an increase in wealth. This is the factor which tends to raise the price of bonds. If it outweighs the factors working in a downward direction a rise in the national income may raise the price of bonds, i.e. lower the interest rate!

It is impossible to assess on *a priori* grounds alone the extent to which this is mere theoretical *curiosum*. But even if empirical considerations ruled the possibility out of court it would still serve as a reminder of the important point that a general change in income affects the demand for bonds not only by altering the demand for money but also by altering the supply of the other alternative to bonds —the income deriving from the ownership of real assets. In a downswing, for example, the income from real assets decreases while the amount of interest on the public debt may change little or not at all. This can well constitute too important a change in the relative supply of different assets to deserve neglect. Again, in considering the determinants of long-term trends in interest rates on Government securities it would be a great mistake to consider only the growth in the money stock and in the debt.

The introduction of national income and of the income

44

from real assets thus yields an important point in the theory of the price of bonds. In addition, however, it has provided us with a theory of the yield of real assets, or rather its inverse Q, the price of £1 of income from real assets. The solution for Q of the equations given above is

$$Q = \frac{M[(1-a)(N-cN-d)-(aN+b)]-Y[j(N-cN-d)+f(aN+b)]}{(N-cN-d)(aR+k)+(aN+b)(cR+e)}$$

Once again, the five propositions enunciated in Chapter I hold. Q will be raised by a fall in the income from real assets, a shift in preferences towards real assets, a redistribution of assets in favour of those whose desire to hold real assets is particularly strong, an increase in the quantity of money or by a decreased desire to hold money.

The solution for Q shows that given Y, Q is a function of the three variables, M, N and R. If attention is concentrated upon each one in turn on a *ceteris paribus* basis it might be said that we have a liquidity preference theory, a bond preference theory and a real asset preference theory respectively of the price of income from real assets or its reciprocal, their yield. Thus if Y, N and R are assumed to remain constant a diagram can be drawn showing the yield of real assets (the reciprocal of Q) as a decreasing function of the quantity of money. This 'constant income from real assets and constant number of bonds liquidity preference curve' rests on the same basis and therefore is as valid or invalid as the curve which relates the yield of bonds (the reciprocal of H) to the quantity of money. The liquidity preference theory, then, works as well for real assets as it does for bonds.

This analysis of Q can be expressed alternatively in terms of the price level of real assets. Let us define J as an index of this price level such that multiplying it by a constant, K, gives the total value of all real assets. K is

45

therefore a measure of the total volume of these assets, but since we are not going to discuss changes in it there is no need to touch upon the thorny problems of measuring capital.

The total value of all real assets is also equal to the product of the income deriving from their ownership, R, and the value of £1 of such income, Q. Hence JK = RQ so that:

$$J = \frac{RQ}{K}$$

Substituting this into the solution for Q gives:

$$J = \frac{M[(1-a)\ (N-cN-d)-c(aN+b)]-Y[j(N-c-d)+f(aN+b)]}{K\left[(N-cN-d)\left(a+\dfrac{k}{R}\right)+(aN+b)\left(c+\dfrac{e}{R}\right)\right]}$$

In order to discuss the interpretation of this equation it is necessary to explain a limitation upon it which results from the simple linear form in which the asset demand equations were expressed. Suppose that the quantity of money, M, and the number of bonds, N, were twice as great and that as a result the price level was also twice as great, the real value of all the variables remaining the same. National income, Y, and the income from real assets, R, would then be twice as large. It is clear that under these circumstances the price level of real assets would also be twice as great while the yields Q and H would be the same. Everything would thus be twice as great in nominal terms but unchanged in real terms. Now this is not apparent from the equations, which appear to suggest that doubling M, N, Y and R would alter Q and would not double J. The reason for this is that the equations are linear approximations which only hold for small changes, so that large changes would alter the values of the parameters. Consider, for example, the coefficient d which gives the increment in the value of bonds demanded with a unit change in H, the inverse of the yield on bonds. If prices were twice as high d would have to be twice as great as well in order for a given change in H to have the same effect in real terms. The same applies to the coefficients b, k and e. If M, N, Y and R doubled, d, b, k and e would all double too and so, therefore, would J. Hence the apparent inconsistency is resolved.

Remembering, then, that the equation for J only is a linear approximation, let us see what it tells us. *Ceteris paribus*, J, the price level of real estate, factories, and businesses of all sorts will clearly in increased by (1) a rise in the quantity of money, M, (2) a fall in the level of income, Y, and in the income from real assets, R, or (3) a shift in asset preferences away from money and bonds towards such assets.

These propositions hold equally well in an economy where the private sector holds no bonds which are liabilities of the monetary sector, i.e. where there is no privately held national debt. Under these circumstances N, b, c, d, e and f are all zero and the solution for J reduces to:

$$J = \frac{M(1 - a) - jY}{K\left(a + \dfrac{k}{R}\right)}$$

Although the bulk of the discussion concentrates on bond prices it has now been shown that the approach of this book is not limited to the analysis of bond prices. The theory applies to underdeveloped countries as well as to overdeveloped countries. If, for example, the three main types of asset widely held are money, gold (sold on a free market) and real estate, the analysis provides a vehicle for explaining movements in the price of gold and the price level of real estate.

One complication remains to be discussed in this chap-

47

ter. The assumption was made in setting up the asset demand functions that there is a given relationship between national money income and the price level. It obviously makes some difference what this relationship is, so we shall examine the two extreme cases. One possibility is that the price level moves proportionately with national income and the income from real assets so that real income is unchanged, while the other extreme is that the price level is constant so that nominal and real incomes alter proportionately.

Suppose that the price level, national income and the income from real assets all rise by 10 per cent. This has two effects. Firstly, it lowers total wealth in real terms by reducing the real value of the private sector's holding of money and bonds. This reduction in wealth will reduce the demand in real terms for all three assets but since the actual loss is concentrated on money and bonds the result will be a tendency to shift into these two assets out of real assets. Hence the first effect is that the price per £1 of income from real assets, Q, must fall relatively to both H and money.

Secondly, the rise in the volume of transactions with an unchanged real income will raise the demand for money relatively to the demand for bonds and real assets. They must therefore fall in price relatively to money. Adding these two effects, it appears that Q and H must both fall, Q more than H. In other words, the postulated change in prices and incomes will raise the yield on bonds and raise the yield on real assets even more.

Now take the other extreme, where a rise in national income and the income from real assets is unaccompanied by any change in the price level. The argument proceeds along the same lines except that in this case total wealth in real terms is increased instead of decreased. The first effect, the wealth effect, will be an attempt on the part of

48

wealth owners to hold some of their increased wealth in the form of money and bonds, so that real asset prices, Q, will have to fall relatively to bonds and money. The second effect will be an increased demand for money both because of a rise in the volume of transactions and because of the increase in real income. This will necessitate a rise in the yield of bonds and real assets, i.e. a fall in H and Q. Hence the total effect will be, as before, a fall in Q and a smaller fall in H.

A change in money national income and the income from real assets will therefore have effects in the same direction whether or not the price level also rises. There is no reason to suppose that the magnitude of the effects will not depend upon the amount of price change, however, so that it is important to remember that the price level and real income are relevant to interest rate determination as well as nominal income.

The theory has been expounded as an aggregative version of the general theory sketched in Chapter I. It can also be regarded as a development and extension of the liquidity preference theory of interest with the quantities of all assets, not just money, given their rightful place in the analysis.[1]

The theory relates to stock equilibrium at a moment of time, given the existing amounts of various assets and given the level of money income and the price level. It is thus a static partial analysis of the demand side of asset price formation. While it relates to the impact of changes

[1] Mrs Robinson's paper 'The rate of interest' (in *Econometrica* 1950, reprinted in her book *The Rate of Interest and Other Essays*) approaches the problem along similar lines, as is evident from her remark that 'there is no such thing as *the* rate of interest and . . . the demand and supply of every type of asset has just as much right to be considered as the demand and supply of money' (at the beginning of Section 2 of her paper). The present work lays more stress on real assets than Mrs Robinson does, and presents a more rigorous analysis.

in the stock of assets or in income and the price level upon asset prices, it contains nothing about the supply of assets or about effects proceeding in the other direction, from asset prices to national income and the price level. Thus it is no more than one part of a general theory of employment, asset prices and money. The construction of such a general theory would require several other parts: an analysis of the supply of assets, of the demand and supply of the factors of production and of the demand and supply of current output.

V

THE CONSOLIDATION OF THE
PRIVATE SECTOR

THE analysis presented so far has regarded bonds and real assets as two homogeneous assets each with a single yield. If instead we take bonds to mean all negotiable debt issued by the monetary sector and abandon the assumption that real assets are homogeneous, the prices of the two kinds of assets become averages of some sort. Changes in the composition of either of these composite assets may then affect their average price even in the absence of any change in preferences or in total quantities. A reduction in the average maturity of bonds (the national debt), for instance, may change the average yield of bonds.

The necessity of overlooking such complications in order to achieve the simplicity requisite for analysis is well recognized. The sort of aggregation involved is not peculiar to the theory of asset prices but is a commonplace. Its limitations and significance are of a perfectly ordinary sort.

The analysis also contains aggregation of a different kind, which is less usual and therefore deserves some discussion. This is the cancelling out of assets and liabilities which are purely internal to a sector. Whereas the inclusion of, for example, both bills and long-term securities in 'bonds' merely ignores the differences between bills and long-term securities, the consolidation of the balance sheets of a creditor and a debtor results in the total disappearance of the debt. Thus while the aggregation of assets simplifies the characteristics of debts, the aggregation of debtors and creditors altogether removes some debts from the analysis, something which is rather harder to swallow.

In the present case the consolidation into the private sector of all households, firms and institutions outside the monetary sector excludes from the analysis any explicit consideration of the relatively enormous amounts of paper assets which are purely internal to the private sector. This may seem unacceptable at first sight. A great deal of this private debt is, after all, a close substitute for much of the public debt and interest rates on the two tend to vary together. How then can it be right to include the quantity of public debt (bonds) and exclude the quantity of private debt from the analysis? The present chapter seeks to provide an answer to this problem.

The question is not whether the pattern of private indebtedness is relevant in the analysis of interest rates on private debt; clearly it is relevant. The problem is whether private indebtedness affects the price of assets which are net assets of the private sector as a whole—bonds and real assets in the exposition of the previous chapter. Will not a change in private indebtedness or a change in preferences for private debt affect the price of bonds?

Let us start to answer the question by examining the effects of an assumed change in the pattern of private indebtedness. Suppose for example that a law is passed which states that Mr Jones owes Mr Smith a large sum of money. Whether or not Mr Jones immediately discharges this debt, the rise in Mr Smith's wealth and the fall in Mr Jones' need not exert exactly equal and opposite effects on their holdings of money, bonds and real assets. If Mr Smith always holds a larger fraction of his net wealth in the form of real assets than Mr Jones does, the demand for real assets of the private sector as a whole will rise. Thus the change in intrasector indebtedness is reflected in the aggregate asset demand.

Now consider a more significant change. Suppose that limited liability has not hitherto existed and is now introduced. Business owners therefore incorporate their businesses, sell some of the equity and buy shares in other businesses, a stock exchange being founded. The owners of businesses therefore achieve greater liquidity and lower risk, through the marketability of shares and the diversification of holdings. Furthermore shares now constitute a new form in which wealth can be held by those wealth owners who previously held only money and bonds. The result of all this is that share prices appear as a new variable in the demand functions for other assets, that wealth owners now demand shares as well as other assets and that limited liability companies now constitute a new and additional class of wealth owners.

It is clear that the demand of the private sector for money, bonds and real assets will not be unaffected by these changes. Nonetheless, demand functions of the private sector as a whole, which do not include share prices among the determinants of demand can still be constructed. The demand for bonds, for example, is written as a function of the prices only of bonds and real assets by supposing that at each possible combination of these prices the prices of shares are such as to equate the demand and supply of shares. The form of the bond demand function is therefore the same as it was before, say

$$D_N = cW + dH + eQ + fY$$

but it must be interpreted slightly differently. Thus d now gives the effect on the demand for bonds of

(1) a change in H; and
(2) the change in share prices which precisely offsets the

disequilibrium in the share market caused by that change in H;

given W, A and Y. In other words, d now reflects not only the direct effect of a change in H but also its indirect effect via the market in equities.

Similar complications apply in the case of the other co-efficients in the asset demand functions. Consider f in the bond demand function for instance. A rise in the level of income Y, by raising the demand for money will cause people to try to sell bonds and real assets. The direct effect on the demand for bonds is included in f, the indirect effect induced by any change in the yield of real assets is given by e. But a second indirect effect will also appear: people will try to sell shares which will lower their price and hence react upon the demand for bonds since shares are a sub-stitute for bonds. Since this effect is not treated explicitly, it must be included in f. This coefficient therefore gives the effect upon the demand for bonds of both:

(1) a change in income; and
(2) the change in share prices which offsets the excess demand or supply of shares caused by the change in income.[1]

These examples of changes in the pattern of private indebtedness lead us to the conclusion that given asset preferences, such changes may alter the aggregate asset demand functions of the private sector. These functions depend not only upon preferences in respect of inter-sector assets but also upon preferences concerning intra-sector assets and upon the amounts of such assets in existence.

[1] Share prices could naturally be included as one of the independent variables in the asset demand equations, but while this might be useful if one of these functions were being studied in isolation, it would not be useful in the present context, for then the price level of shares would have to be treated as an additional exogenous variable along with M, N, Y and R.

So far the discussion has dealt with purely exogenous changes in the pattern of intrasector liabilities and assets without any examination of the determinants of this pattern. This problem will be taken up in Chapter VI. Meanwhile, we must take account of the fact that these liabilities and assets are relevant to the demand for money, bonds and real assets in another way. Let us turn from imagined changes produced by some *deus ex machina* to the effects of changes in asset preferences.

Suppose again that shares exist, constituting a purely intra-private-sector asset and liability. Suppose that share-owners in general suffer a change in preferences such that for any given level of wealth they all wish to hold fewer shares and more of all other assets than before. Share prices will fall, which will both inhibit this (by causing owners to hang on to their shares) and enable it to take place to some extent (by inducing others to buy them up). In the end result, the reduction in the price of shares, the fall in the wealth of shareholders and the changed pattern of share ownership may alter the relative demands for money, bonds and real assets so that bond prices or real asset prices change. Thus a change in preferences which does not directly alter the demand for, say, bonds relatively to money may do so indirectly. We have just seen, however, that in our two-sector model the demand function for bonds should be interpreted so as to include indirect influences of this sort. It follows that if bond prices are lowered by the change in demand for shares one of the coefficients in the bond demand function must have altered so as to lower the value of D_N for any given combination of W, H, Q and Y.

A change in asset preferences may relate exclusively to intra-private-sector paper assets. All other changes in asset preferences can be dealt with in terms of the factors made explicit in the model. Suppose, for instance, that there is a change in asset preferences such that at any given set of prices both firms and households desire to switch from bonds to shares but there is no change in the demand for money or real assets. Let us leave out the shares, which are not explicitly mentioned in the model, and express what has happened by saying that other things remaining unchanged, the demand for bonds has fallen. Consequently their price will fall.

The case just considered concerned an alteration of preferences away from bonds and toward shares, with the demand for money initially unaffected. Suppose instead that there is a shift from money to shares with no change in the demand for bonds or real assets. This will raise the price of bonds and real assets. The reason for this is that the effect of raising the demand for shares will be to raise their price so that both households and firms will seek to buy bonds and real assets which will then have become relatively higher yielding. Hence in this case the price of bonds and real assets changes because of a change in the demand for money. Once again the matter can be expressed perfectly well in consolidated terms: the demand for money is reduced while the demand for bonds and real assets is unchanged; money must therefore fall in price relatively to bonds and real assets and since the price of money is unity this means that their prices increase.

We are left with changes in asset preferences which do not relate to money, bonds or real assets but only to intra-private-sector debt. These changes in preferences, in contrast to those just discussed, involve no direct alteration in the demand for money, bonds and real assets. Nonetheless they will have some effect on the price levels of bonds and real assets though not a large one. An example will illustrate this.

Suppose that a large number of English households suffer an alteration in their preferences with respect to

56

building society shares and deposits with finance houses so that in the absence of any changes in interest rates they would withdraw funds on a large scale from building societies and deposit them instead with suppliers of hire-purchase finance. The immediate impact of this upon the prices of marketable Government securities will be limited to the net effect of (a) sales of Government securities by building societies to compensate for the loss of funds and (b) purchases by finance houses to maintain the ratio of their marketable assets to deposits. The resulting effect on the gilt-edged market will be smaller than the tightening in the mortgage market and the easing in the market for hire-purchase finance, whether these movements are reflected in alterations in interest rates or in other ways such as changes in repayment periods.

These then are the primary effects of the change in preferences. There will be secondary effects as well, however, and still other tertiary and quaternary repercussions. Consider, for example, the second round of effects, supposing, to simplify exposition, that interest rates rather than the other terms of credit contracts respond to changes in demand and supply. The rise in mortgage rates may induce some investors (c) to switch from Government paper to the mortgage market and some borrowers (d) to sell gilt-edged rather than mortgage their property. The rise in the interest rates offered by building societies may (e) induce some selling of Government securities while the fall in the rates paid by finance houses will (f) have the opposite effect.

There is no need to carry the story any farther. The point emerges that the net effect of all these adjustments of assets and liabilities will be relatively small so far as the prices of Government securities are concerned. Each factor tending to raise their prices will be faced with some factor working in the opposite direction. Thus effects (a) and (b), as pointed out above, will partly counteract one another; so will (c), (d), (e) and (f). The major effects of the change in preferences are confined to the markets for intra-private-sector credit and there is no substantial effect upon the price level of bonds.

These examples show that a change in the pattern of private indebtedness or preferences for intra-private-sector assets may affect the prices of bonds or real assets. They also show that while the pattern of private indebtedness does not enter into the analysis explicitly it does so implicitly, so that the analysis is fully capable of dealing with the effects of these changes. Thus it turns out that the aggregation involved in the consolidation of balance sheets is not so different from other aggregation. Consider the consumption function, for example, on the supposition that consumption depends on the level of income and on its distribution. If the distribution of income is not taken into explicit account it can be dealt with implicitly. The marginal propensity to consume then gives the effect upon consumption of both

(1) a change in the level of income; and
(2) the redistribution of income occasioned by that change in its level.

Changes in the income distribution otherwise occasioned will alter the value of the marginal propensity to consume. All this is analogous to what has been said here about asset demands.

We have now given a logical answer to the puzzle of why the vast amounts of paper assets which are internal to the private sector are excluded from explicit mention in the analysis. This answer is, in brief, that in an aggregative model of asset price formation the only assets whose prices can be treated as endogenous variables are those which are net assets of one or other of the sectors.

This is true simply because each sector is treated as if it were a single behaviour unit. Consequently the quantities of those assets which are entirely liabilities of the sector within which they are held need not appear in the analysis. Changes in preferences concerning them and autonomous changes in their structure will be reflected in the demand functions for the assets entering explicitly into the analysis.

VI

APPLYING THE THEORY

THE theory has so far been expounded in abstract terms. It is now time to see how it can be applied. This will be done here by using the statistics of financial assets and liabilities in the U.S. in the post-war period put out by the Federal Reserve System as part of their Flow of Funds studies.[1] The decision to use these statistics and to treat the average yield on the public debt as the variable to be 'explained' is based solely on considerations of convenience. Had the necessary information been available, the price of gold in Turkey or the average yield on real assets in Denmark would have served equally well as an example. The point is that the theory as stated above cannot be directly applied to particular circumstances without modification and that the nature of the modification required will vary from case to case. Modification would be unnecessary only if the theory were to be applied to an economy where the net wealth of the private sector consisted exclusively of money, bonds and real assets.

Modification of a simple theory in order to make use of it is frequently necessary. The most obvious example is the simple theory of income determination where national income is defined as the sum of consumption and investment. Since the social accounts of most countries define national income as including various other items as well,

[1] The major reference is the volume *Flow of Funds in the United States 1939-53*. The figures given here, however, come from later tabulations which use a revised sector and asset classification. Still more recent figures have appeared in the *Federal Reserve Bulletin*, August 1959.

the theory cannot be applied until it is modified appropriately. What is appropriate depends upon the nature of the available statistics rather than upon any abstract considerations. If, for instance, there are figures only of gross income and investment, but not of net income and investment, then the theory which is used to explain these and related magnitudes must be couched in terms of gross income. The possibility that net income might be more appropriate theoretically is irrelevant if no measure of it is available.

In the example chosen the statistics are plentiful. In the Flow of Funds studies twelve sectors, some of them divided into subsectors, and eighteen types of paper assets, some of them subdivided, are distinguished. What we need to do here is to group together two groups of sectors and a few groups of assets.

For our monetary sector we take the two Flow of Funds sectors 'Federal Government' and 'Commercial banking and monetary sector'. The sector therefore includes the Federal Government and practically all its agencies, corporations and trust funds (including the Exchange Stabilization Fund and the postal savings system), the Federal Reserve System and the commercial banks. The other sector, the private sector, covers the rest of the economy: households, businesses, charities, state and local government, the rest of the world and financial intermediaries such as insurance companies, mutual savings banks, finance companies and brokers.

This gives American institutional content to our two sectors. To describe all of the private sector's net monetary assets as either money or bonds is hardly possible, however, and we must allow for the fact that the private sector also has some net monetary liabilities to the monetary sector. It is therefore necessary to adopt a new classification of paper assets and liabilities, neglecting all those

61

which are entirely intrasectoral (such as savings and loan association deposits which are both held and owed within the private sector) since we are concerned only with the consolidated assets and liabilities of the private sector treated as a unit. The following classification is suggested.

Money. Currency, demand deposits at commercial banks, time deposits at commercial banks and deposits in the postal savings system. The small amount of deposits of the Federal Reserve System which is held outside the monetary sector is included here.

U.S. Savings Bonds. It is worth while distinguishing these from other Federal debt since they are available and redeemable in unlimited amounts (to the private sector as a whole) on fixed terms. Thus for this part of its debt the monetary authorities have infinitely elastic demand and supply curves.

Federal Obligations. Covers all marketable securities of the Treasury and of Federal agencies and some nonmarketable securities other than savings bonds.

Long-term Debt. State and local obligations, corporate bonds, mortgages, loans by various Federal agencies for housing, farms and business and Government loans to the rest of the world.

Bank Loans.

Miscellaneous. All the other financial items distinguished in the Flow of Funds tables excluding gold.

Table III can now be obtained by consolidating the Flow of Funds table of 'Financial Assets and Liabilities'. The figures relate to the end of 1956 and are all in billions of dollars. They are the same for both sectors with the sign reversed, being based on the assets and liabilities of the monetary sector. If instead figures based on records relating to the private sector had been used, there would have been a minor difference reflecting mail float (items in transit). The table, it should also be noted, makes one

APPLYING THE THEORY

TABLE III

Asset	Sector	
	Monetary	Private
Money	− 194·6	+ 194·6
Savings Bonds	− 55·8	+ 55·8
Federal Obligations	− 84·5	+ 84·5
Long-term Debt	+ 61·5	− 61·5
Bank Loans	+ 67·7	− 67·7
Miscellaneous	− 3·6	+ 3·6
Real Assets	?	?

minor omission in that the capital of commercial banks should be included as a liability of the monetary sector.

There is a more important omission. A great deal of intrasector debt is guaranteed by the monetary sector, primarily mortgages insured or guaranteed by the Veterans' Administration and the Federal Housing Administration. Such a mortgage is as safe an asset as a Federal obligation. It is as though the mortgagee had lent his money to the Government and the Government had lent it, on exactly similar terms, to the mortgagor[1]; if the latter defaults the mortgagee is hardly affected. From the point of view of asset price formation considered aggregatively, Government lending financed by the issue of Federal obligations is equivalent to the Government guarantee of similar private lending. Thus the total amount of Federally insured and guaranteed loans outstanding should be added to the asset item, Federal obligations, and to the liability item, long-term debt. For the end of 1956, the amount in question

[1] I am indebted to Milton Friedman for this point.

63

was about 35·5 billion dollars,[1] so that in the table the items should stand at 120 billions and 92 billions respectively.

In the simple model of Chapter IV bonds were the only interest-yielding paper asset. They are now replaced by two assets and two liabilities. As a rough first approximation we may assume that the monetary sector fixes the yield, but not the amount, of savings bonds and of bank loans and the amount, but not the yield, of Federal obligations and its holding of long-term debt. The asset demand and supply curves of the monetary sector are thus assumed to be either of infinite or of zero elasticity. This assumption now enables us to specify the way in which the supply of assets is given if the miscellaneous item is ignored. For the purposes of the analysis the following are treated as independent variables:

(a) the sum of the quantity of money and the amount of savings bonds outstanding less the amount of bank loans outstanding;

(b) the quantity of Federal obligations outstanding;

(c) the quantity of long-term debt held by the monetary sector[2];

(d) the interest yield or cost which the private sector obtains or pays on money, savings bonds and bank loans—i.e. the terms of issue and redemption of savings bonds, the rate of interest paid on time deposits and the availability and terms of bank loans;

(e) the quantity of real assets;

(f) the level of national income.

---

[1] This figure relates to the two items which account for the great bulk of such guarantees and insurance: F.H.A. housing loan insurance outstanding and the contingent liability of the V.A. on mortgage guarantees.

[2] If the amount of bank loans outstanding were treated as an independent variable it would be included along with long-term debt instead of in item (a) and the interest cost of bank loans need not be included in item (d).

The amounts of Federal obligations, long-term debt and real assets can be expressed in terms of the income which their ownership confers if this be convenient. Otherwise the quantities of paper assets can be measured by their nominal values and the quantity of real assets at market value or, in the case of reproducible assets, at replacement cost.

With this list of exogenous factors, and with a given asset and liability demand function of the private sector, the following are determined, i.e. constitute the dependent variables:

(g) the composition of money plus savings bonds less bank loans;

(h) the price level of Federal obligations and its inverse, the average yield of Federal obligations;

(i) the price level of long-term debt and its inverse, the average yield of long-term debt;

(j) the price level of real assets and its inverse, their yield.

One of the differences between these two sets of variables and the smaller number in the theoretical analysis of Chapter IV is that the independent variables include a net liability, long-term debt, as well as some net assets. Thus some assumptions about liabilities are made necessary, assumptions comparable with those that all assets are substitutes for money and are superior with respect to wealth.

A priori it seems difficult to say whether, *ceteris paribus*, a rise in wealth will make the private sector want to borrow more on long-term, creating an excess stock supply of long-term debt by the private sector, or whether the effect will be in the opposite direction. If the latter is the case, the effect of a rise in its wealth is to induce the private sector to attempt to repay debt. The direction of the substitution effect, on the other hand, is clear: a fall in the rate of interest on debt will make being in debt less undesirable, while a rise will lead debtors to endeavour to repay their debts. We shall assume that if the wealth effect of a change in the price level of long-term debt goes in the opposite direction to the substitution effect, the latter dominates. In other words we suppose that, *ceteris paribus*, a fall in the price-level of long-term debts reduces the net amount of it which the private sector desires to have outstanding.

Another complication which deserves note is that the figures in Table III include some of the dollar assets and liabilities of the rest of the world. The factors which regulate the composition of the rest of the world's net dollar assets are partly different from those relevant to the bulk of the private sector, for instance in the case of intergovernmental borrowing. None the less, there is presumably some substitutability between dollar assets owned by the rest of the world so that even though their asset demand curves may move rather differently from those of the domestic private sector, they do at least slope downwards in the same way.

We can now set out the factors which will cause the dependent variables to change. As before, let us pick out the price level of Federal obligations for consideration and list the effect which changes in the independent variables will have upon it. For convenience the following statements are formulated in terms of the average yield of Federal obligations. *Ceteris paribus*, this average will be:

(*a*) lowered by an increase in the sum of the quantity of money and the amount of savings bonds less the amount of bank loans outstanding;

(*b*) raised by an increase in the quantity of Federal obligations outstanding;

(*c*) lowered by an increase in the monetary sector's holding of long-term debt, since such an increase would lower interest rates on long-term debts and these are substitutes for Federal obligations;

(d) raised by an increase in the interest rates paid on time deposits, postal savings deposits and savings bonds and charged on bank loans;

(e) either raised or lowered by an increase in the income from real assets, the assumptions made do not enable us to say which;

(f) raised by an increase in the national income, given the income from real assets.

These statements all follow from the assumption of a given structure of demand. It is obvious, however, that if this structure changes, the average yield on Federal obligations will alter even in the absence of any changes in any of the six independent variables. Four possible causes of shifts in the demand functions deserve to have attention drawn to them. One is that expectations change. If a significant proportion of wealth owners base their portfolio decisions partly upon anticipations of future changes in asset prices, changes in these anticipations will obviously have an effect on the wealth owner's asset demands. Where, for instance, scepticism about a cheap money policy turns into a conviction that the monetary authorities are going to succeed in achieving their aims for some years, the demand for Federal obligations will be raised. Where, on the other hand, a generally anticipated fall in interest rates fails to materialize, so that interest expectations are revised upward, the demand for Federal obligations will be reduced. It is difficult to say much in general terms about the formation of expectations, but these examples show how important expectations can be in affecting interest rates.

A second reason why asset demands may shift is likely to be unimportant in the short run but of great significance over long periods of time. This is the development of new forms of debt and new financial institutions inside the private sector. From a formal viewpoint the effects of such changes constitute an alteration of the asset preferences of the consolidated private sector. If, for example, the growth of financial intermediaries raises the liquidity of the private sector, there will presumably be some fall in the demand for money as a result. Hence institutional developments will cause trend movements in asset demands. Chapter VII contains some discussion of the importance of financial intermediaries so all that is necessary here is to remind the reader of this source of changes in demand.

Another cause of changes in the average yield on Federal obligations which will make itself felt through a shift in the private sector's asset demand functions is an alteration in the average quality of Federal obligations. These include a wide range of securities from bills to bonds, from fully taxable securities to wholly exempt ones. At some times the monetary authorities may peg the price of long-term securities while at other times they may be liable to extensive capital gains and losses. A change in maturity structure, tax status or debt policy can make Federal obligations in general more or less attractive, lowering or raising their average yield even in the absence of any alteration in the other determinants of this average.

Fourthly, the tax structure exerts an influence upon asset demands. In the United States, for example, interest and the income from real assets are taxed more heavily than capital gains, while the convenience yield from money and from owner-used durables is not taxed at all. Thus a change in the general level of taxation will alter the relative attractiveness of different assets and affect their prices. At the present level of aggregation any detailed discussion of this matter would be otiose; the only relationship which can usefully be considered for the private sector regarded as a unit is the effect of the general height of income (and capital gains) taxation upon the choice between assets with a monetary yield and assets with a convenience yield.

Let us suppose that the exogenous factors listed above (a) to (f) are given, that expectations are given and that the composition of the stock of Federal obligations is given. Let there be a general increase in income tax rates to finance an increase in Government expenditure which is not of such a sort that individual wealth owners regard themselves as directly and individually benefited by it. How will asset demands react? The answer is that there will be a substitution effect and a wealth effect. The former will be in the direction of shifting out of money-yielding assets into convenience-yielding assets. The wealth effect, on the other hand, will work in the opposite direction; the fall in the income from money-yielding assets is equivalent to a reduction in holdings of such assets and hence in total wealth. This lowers the demand for all superior assets, including convenience-yielding assets whose quantity is, by assumption, unchanged so that taken by itself the wealth effect would induce a shift out of convenience-yielding assets into money-yielding assets. Thus on balance an increase in the general level of taxation of the sort specified may either raise or lower the average yield on Federal obligations.

The theory has now been stated. Its variables are all measurable not merely in principle, but also in practice; with one exception (real assets) the various assets and liabilities have been defined in terms of Flow of Funds statistics. Hence the theory has been set out in a way which makes it relevant to a particular case, namely the United States in the post-war period. We have used it to produce a series of propositions about the determinants of the average yield on Federal obligations. It is apparent that we could use it to provide a similar set of propositions concerning the average yield or price level of real assets. If real assets had been divided into a number of categories, more detailed propositions could be made though this might require the introduction of considerable complications.

The propositions put forward all have the same status as those enumerated in the model of Chapter IV. They stem from simple assumptions about the demand for assets applied to a particular aggregative treatment of a particular institutional framework. It is not claimed that this treatment is the only possible one, since even with the same two-fold sector division there are alternative ways of grouping assets and liabilities. None the less, the analysis provides a theory which, whether right or wrong, is at least directly relevant to the real world. It is therefore testable.

The remainder of this chapter describes an attempt at statistical testing of the theory. Since I have no competence in econometrics, and since only a few regressions out of many possible ones have been computed, the results should be regarded as no more than a demonstration that the approach is worth while. Too much importance should not be attached to the values of the coefficients in the absence of more refined analysis.

In principle, the variable to be explained should be the average yield to maturity on Federal obligations held by the private sector. As an approximation of this we take a weighted average of four interest rates on U.S. Government taxable securities which are published regularly in the *Federal Reserve Bulletin*: the rates on new issues of Treasury bills, 9–12-month issues, 3–5-year issues and long-term bonds.[1] These were weighted 1, 2, 3 and 4 respectively in order to achieve a rough reflection of the average

[1] The old series. The figure for December 1957 was estimated at 3·3 per cent on the basis of the new series.

maturity structure of the debt held by the private sector as revealed by *Treasury Ownership Surveys* for the middle of the period examined. We denote this average yield by I.

The main source of data for the explanatory variables was the mimeographed Flow of Funds material put out by the Federal Reserve Board. The 'Liabilities and Assets' tables relate to the end of December of each year, but for 1952 onward figures for the end of March, June and September were obtainable through use of the quarterly 'Sources and Uses' tables. In some cases there was a small discrepancy between the figure obtained for, say, September by adding the flows of the first three quarters' figures for last December and that obtained by subtracting the flow of the last figure for next December. These discrepancies, which presumably result from errors of rounding and which were in no case large, were resolved arbitrarily. The three series obtained were:

(*a*) the sum of the quantity of money and the amount of savings bonds outstanding less the amount of bank loans outstanding, denoted by N;

(*b*) the quantity of Federal obligations outstanding, FO;

(*c*) the monetary sector's holding of long-term debt (defined as in Table III except for the exclusion of Government loans to the rest of the world), denoted by LTD.

In accordance with the argument above, an estimate of the two major items of Government guarantees of private debt, G, was added both to (*b*) and (*c*) so that these variables become FO + G and LTD + G.[1]

[1] F.H.A. housing loan insurance outstanding end December up to 1953 from Table A17 in Saulnier, Halcrow and Jacoby, *Federal Lending and Loan Insurance*, thereafter from a letter from the F.H.A. division of research and statistics. Contingent liability of the V.A. on guaranteed mortgage debt end December up to 1953 from Table A10, op. cit., thereafter estimated from figures of the amount of V.A. guaranteed mortgage debt appearing in the *Federal Reserve Bulletin*. The figures for the end of March, June and September were interpolated.

TABLE IV

Year	Quarter Ending	I %	FO+G $ bn	LTD+G $ bn	Y $ bn	N $ bn	Q %	P (1954 =100)	T
1945	Dec.	1·48	93·7	21·0	168·2	163·3	1·96	68·0	15·3
1946	Dec.	1·47	86·1	24·5	191·9	174·3	2·01	74·6	16·4
1947	Dec.	1·72	85·2	28·4	206·5	177·7	2·01	85·3	17·2
1948	Dec.	1·83	84·9	35·4	229·2	176·2	2·17	89·5	17·9
1949	Dec.	1·62	88·7	41·5	214·8	178·3	2·15	87·7	16·9
1950	Dec.	1·88	94·6	49·9	261·1	176·6	2·22	91·8	19·2
1951	Dec.	2·23	95·9	56·6	286·0	179·6	2·41	97·5	19·0
1952	Mar.	2·19	97·1	58·1	287·2	175·7	2·49	97·6	18·2
	June	2·17	95·9	59·7	288·0	177·7	2·54	97·7	18·8
	Sept.	2·34	98·1	60·7	292·4	181·2	2·55	98·4	18·9
	Dec.	2·41	99·8	62·3	300·6	182·6	2·56	99·0	19·8
1953	Mar.	2·50	101·6	63·3	306·3	176·9	2·57	98·8	19·4
	June	2·83	102·9	64·4	308·7	178·3	2·64	98·8	19·2
	Sept.	2·62	106·1	67·0	307·2	179·5	2·67	99·2	19·3
	Dec.	2·27	106·8	67·5	300·1	186·5	2·68	99·2	19·7
1954	Mar.	1·85	106·2	68·7	299·3	182·1	2·67	99·9	19·7
	June	1·77	103·3	69·6	299·4	184·5	2·63	99·8	19·7
	Sept.	1·82	104·5	72·4	300·9	188·1	2·62	100·0	19·4
	Dec.	1·95	106·1	72·6	307·5	193·3	2·62	100·2	21·0
1955	Mar.	2·21	108·5	75·1	316·9	188·2	2·62	100·5	20·0
	June	2·31	109·5	76·9	327·3	185·3	2·63	100·9	20·8
	Sept.	2·61	114·5	78·4	335·0	185·0	2·72	101·5	21·1
	Dec.	2·77	117·5	79·8	341·4	186·7	2·77	101·9	21·6
1956	Mar.	2·73	118·9	81·7	342·2	179·5	2·81	102·8	20·8
	June	2·81	116·3	82·4	346·2	178·7	2·88	103·6	21·6
	Sept.	3·22	118·3	85·4	350·8	178·0	2·95	104·8	22·0
	Dec.	3·46	120·0	85·9	357·9	182·7	2·96	105·7	23·3
1957	Mar.	3·30	123·0	87·4	361·5	175·9	3·13	107·0	22·5
	June	3·59	121·4	88·7	364·1	175·5	3·22	107·8	23·1
	Sept.	3·80	124·6	90·3	368·7	175·5	3·41	108·9	24·1
	Dec.	3·16	125·8	92·2	361·5	180·2	3·41	109·4	24·7

Variable (d) listed above is the interest yield or cost obtained or paid on money, savings bonds and time deposits. To measure this a simple average was taken of the rate of interest paid on time deposits by member banks,[1] the yield to maturity on Series E savings bonds and rates on short-term business loans made by banks in nineteen large cities. This average, denoted by Q, rose from 1·96 per cent in December 1945 to 3·41 per cent in December 1957 with hardly any interruption.

Variables (e) and (f) listed above are the quantity of real assets and the level of national income. As was argued earlier, these two are very highly correlated and since in any case the quantity of real assets or the income derived from them is not readily susceptible of measurement on a quarterly basis, national income alone, Y, is taken as a variable. The concept used is the seasonally adjusted quarterly total of national income expressed as an annual rate.[2]

The price index used for deflating the variables, P, is the implicit price deflator in the American national income statistics.[3] Lastly, the variable T is the annual rate of turnover (in the last month of the quarter) of demand deposits except interbank and Government deposits at 338 centres.[4] It was introduced to represent the transactions demand for money in the equations where money income does not enter.

The regressions were computed with seasonal adjust-

[1] Reported for six-monthly periods in the *Federal Reserve Bulletin* whence are also derived the quarterly figures of interest rates on bank loans.

[2] The data are to be found in Table I–9, *U.S. Income and Output*, published by the U.S. Department of Commerce. They were taken from an earlier publication before the quarterly G.N.P. figures were available.

[3] See *U.S. Income and Output*, Table VII–3, 'Implicit price deflator for seasonally adjusted quarterly G.N.P., 1954 = 100'. Annual figures were used for 1945 and 1946 in the absence of quarterly figures for the period before March 1947.

[4] From a mimeographed release by the Board of Governors of the Federal Reserve System, *Bank Debits and Rates of Turnover—Revised Series 1943–52* and the *Federal Reserve Bulletin*. The 338 centres exclude New York and six other large centres. The figures are seasonally unadjusted.

ment factors for March, June and September, but though there is probably some seasonality in the figures this was not strongly marked and it was judged preferable to keep down the number of independent variables. The regressions were, therefore, recomputed without seasonal adjustment, giving the results shown in Table V. The first row, for instance, shows that regression *6·0* has a multiple correlation coefficient of ·96 and that the regression is:

$$I = - \cdot27 - \cdot025\frac{N}{P}\cdot100 + \cdot017\frac{FO+G}{P}\cdot100 - \cdot051\frac{LTD+G}{P}\cdot100 +$$

$$+ \cdot018\frac{Y}{P}\cdot100 + \cdot6Q + \cdot084T$$

It will be seen that three alternative forms of regression have been tried out. In regressions *6·0–7·0*, net liquid assets, Federal obligations, long-term debt and income are taken into account as absolute amounts valued at 1954 prices. In the next two regressions Federal obligations, debt and income are expressed as a fraction of net liquid assets, while in regressions *9·0* and *9·1* assets and liabilities are set in relation to income.

The main feature of the results is that they are all in accord with the theory as set out above, with one exception. Leaving this aside for the minute, let us see that signs and orders of magnitude are consistent with expectation by examining the regressions. First of all, consider the variable Q, the interest rate earned on liquid assets and paid on liquid liabilities. This has a positive coefficient as we should expect, and in all cases its inclusion improves the fit. Excluding it raises the coefficient of the FO + G term in regressions *8·0–8·1* and *9·0–9·1*, perhaps because both FO + G and Q showed an upward trend.

Leaving aside Q, consider equation *7·0*. It is a simple matter to work out the effect on I of various postulated changes in the independent variables. Let us take as a base

74

TABLE V

Regression Coefficients (and Standard Errors)

Regression Number	Multiple Correlation Coefficient (R)	Constant Term	$\frac{N}{P}.100$	$\frac{FO+G}{P}.100$	$\frac{LTD+G}{P}.100$	$\frac{Y}{P}.100$	$\frac{FO+G}{N}$	$\frac{LTD+G}{N}$	$\frac{Y}{N}$	$\frac{FO+G}{Y}$	$\frac{LTD+G}{Y}$	$\frac{N}{Y}$	Q	T
6·0	·96	−·27	−·025 (·0087)	·017 (·009)	−·051 (·0098)	·018 (·0052)							·60 (·46)	·084 (·055)
6·1	·96	−·27	−·023 (·0088)	·015 (·0091)	−·051 (·010)	·020 (·0053)							1·015 (·38)	
6·2	·94	4·21	−·041 (·0066)	·032 (·0073)	−·041 (·01)	·016 (·0057)								
7·0	·96	1·41	−·032 (·0066)	·024 (·0071)	−·048 (·0096)	·016 (·0051)								·13 (·045)
8·0	·96	4·46					2·96 (1·24)	−9·13 (1·79)	3·78 (·63)				·83 (·37)	
8·1	·95	−3·91					4·29 (1·16)	−7·51 (1·75)	3·93 (·68)					
9·0	·95	4·44								3·65 (2·21)	−14·68 (2·90)	−5·73 (1·54)	1·28 (·33)	
9·1	·92	8·14								9·31 (2·07)	−12·48 (3·52)	−10·31 (1·24)		

the position at the end of the third quarter of 1954 when I was 1·82 per cent. (This choice is just a matter of convenience, since P was then 100.) *Ceteris paribus*, an increase in N of say 10 per cent, would have lowered I by ·61 to 1·21 per cent. If the increase in N had been brought about by open market operations, so that the private sector's holding of Federal obligations fell as N rose, interest rates would of course have fallen more, namely by 1·0 to ·82 per cent. Even though the co-efficients of N and FO + G may be subject to considerable error this does bring home the point made in Chapter II that a 'constant number of bonds liquidity preference curve' is very different from an 'open market operations liquidity preference curve'. The results obtained from the other regressions are comparable. A similar calculation performed with *8·1*, for instance, forecasts a drop in I of ·52 and ·91 respectively.

Returning to regression *7·0*, an increase in the amount of long-term debt will lower the yield on Federal obligations. Applying the coefficient — ·048 to a 10 per cent increase in LTD + G, for example, yields a calculated fall of ·35 in I, i.e. a drop to 1·47 per cent. The sign is negative, as the theory suggests, but the magnitude of the effect is implausible. It will be seen that in all the regressions, not only in *7·0*, the long-term debt coefficient is numerically greater than the Federal obligations coefficient by a very substantial amount. This would imply that if the Government borrowed money and lent it, or if it guaranteed more private mortgages so that the LTD + G and FO + G terms rose by equal amounts, the average yield on Federal obligations would fall. This result is not in accord with the theory and constitutes the one unsatisfactory feature of the regressions.

It might be thought that the fact that the volume of Federal guarantees, G, is common to both terms accounts for the relative magnitude of their coefficients. This is not the case, however. Regression *8·1*, for instance, if recomputed with G omitted becomes:

$$I = -3·76 + 4·25\frac{FO}{N} - 11·20\frac{LTD}{N} + 4·07\frac{Y}{N}$$

$$(1·14) \qquad (3·46) \qquad (0·69)$$

with a multiple correlation coefficient of ·955 as against ·954 in the case of *8·1*. The excess of the LTD coefficient over the FO coefficient is actually increased. The explanation of this excess must therefore be sought elsewhere. I am at a loss to provide this explanation. Since the bulk of long-term debt consists of Federal loans, and Federally and bank held mortgages it may well be that the institutional peculiarities of Federal lending and of the mortgage market are relevant.

The effect of a rise in income is, of course, to raise interest rates. If prices, money income and transactions (the rate of turnover of bank deposits) all rose by 10 per cent, regression *7·0* predicts an increase in I of ·89.

Had opportunity permitted, there are various ways in which further manipulation of the data might have improved the fit and provided an explanation of the large size of the LTD + G coefficient.[1] The forms of the regressions and the particular asset classification chosen are arbitrary in the sense that other ones would be equally

[1] Mr Ronald Conley, now a graduate student at The Johns Hopkins University, kindly computed two alternative regressions. One was the same as *8·1* except that first differences were used. The other was also a variation upon *8·1*; savings bonds were included with Federal obligations and bank loans with long-term debt (so that the quantity of money replaced N) and guarantees were omitted. Both regressions had a poorer fit than any in Table V; the first increased the difference between the Federal obligations and long-term debt coefficients while the second reversed the sign of the latter.

consistent with the theory. All that has been done, therefore, is to show the sort of way in which the theory can be formulated to make it apply to a particular problem. It is a theory with two great merits: it is simple and it is testable.

VII

THE PATTERN OF PRIVATE
INDEBTEDNESS

THE net paper assets and liabilities of the private sector
form only a fraction of the total amount of paper assets in
existence. This total includes not only the intersector
assets shown in Table III but also the items which are both
assets and liabilities within the monetary sector and those
which are internal to the private sector. It is this latter
group which is the concern of the present chapter. We shall
examine the forces which affect the nature and amount
of paper assets which are both owed and owned within the
private sector, and then show that although these forces
affect the yield on Federal obligations the analysis of this
book is not invalidated by treating them implicitly rather
than explicitly.

Table VI will serve to give an idea of the orders of
magnitude involved. It is derived from a Flow of Funds
table of assets and liabilities, as was Table III, and all
figures are in (American) billions of dollars at the end of
1956. The first column of figures repeats the information
given in Table III with a more detailed classification of
assets. The second column shows the total amount outstanding of each type of asset net of the amount both
issued and held within the monetary sector. The third
column shows the amount which is both issued and held
within the private sector. Thus the third column registers
the private indebtedness which was consolidated out in the
aggregation of the economy into two sectors and whose

TABLE VI

Asset Classification in Table III	Flow of Funds Asset Classification	Net Assets of Private Sector	Total Outstanding not Internal to Monetary Sector	Difference = Intra Private Sector Debt
Money	Currency and demand deposits	141·0	141·0	—
	Time deposits	53·6	83·7	30·1
Savings bonds	Savings bonds	55·8	55·8	—
Federal obligations	Federal obligations	84·5	84·5	—
Long-term debt	State and local government obligations	− 13·5	50·5	37·0
	Corporate bonds	− 1·3	66·6	65·3
	Mortgages	− 28·3	144·7	116·4
	Federal 'other loans'	− 18·4	18·4	—
Bank loans	Security credit	− 4·3	9·0	4·7
	Consumer credit	− 14·6	42·1	27·5
	Bank loans n.e.c.	− 48·8	48·8	—
Miscellaneous	Other loans (except Federal)	− 1·8	11·4	9·6
	Savings and loan and credit union shares	*	− 40·0	40·0
	Trade credit	·2	76·5	76·3
	Savings through life insurance	2·9	66·4	63·5
	Misc. financial transactions	− 2·7	5·1	2·4
	Misc. deposits	5·0	19·2	14·2
	Corporate stock	*1	338·0	338·0
Real assets	Real assets	?	—	—

[1] Equity in commercial banks.

structure forms the subject of the following discussion. It is convenient to call it private indebtedness even though it includes corporate stock which is not usually referred to as debt.

A great deal of private debt is the liability of non-bank

financial intermediaries. These may be loosely defined as institutions or persons whose assets are primarily paper assets and whose liabilities are large in relation to their assets. Savings banks, insurance companies, building societies, finance companies and investment trusts are all financial intermediaries. So are commercial banks, the Federal Reserve System and some Federal lending institutions, but as these are in the monetary sector we are not concerned with them here. Corporations exercise some of the functions of financial intermediaries in so far as they grant more trade credit than they receive, but this is a minor part of their balance sheets and they are therefore not counted as financial intermediaries.

Let us assume away the presence of financial intermediaries and of financial intermediation in general within the private sector, by supposing that no one who has liabilities held by someone within the sector holds as assets any private liabilities. This means, conversely, that no one whose assets include the liabilities of someone in the private sector is himself a private debtor. In other words all households, firms and other institutions within the private sector are either debtors or creditors so far as intrasector assets are concerned. Under these conditions, the following identity holds, where 'wealth' means net worth and 'sectoral assets' is taken to include all items which are net assets of liabilities of the private sector taken as a whole:

$$
\begin{aligned}
\text{Private indebtedness} &= \text{private debtors' sectoral assets} - \\
&\quad \text{private debtors' wealth} \\
&= \text{private creditors' wealth} - \\
&\quad \text{private creditors' sectoral assets.}
\end{aligned}
$$

It is evident that if no one held sectoral assets to a greater value than his wealth, i.e. if all wealth is held in the form of sectoral assets, private indebtedness will be zero.

Private indebtedness would reach a maximum, equal in amount to the aggregate wealth of the private sector if no holder of sectoral assets had any wealth, i.e. if no one with a positive net worth held any sectoral assets at all. Thus given the distribution of wealth, private indebtedness is raised by a transfer of sectoral assets to wealth owners who hold an amount in excess of their wealth. Four major instances of this may be listed as follows:

(a) house purchase or business expansion financed by mortgages which are not acquired by the monetary sector;

(b) the incorporation of private businesses, i.e. the creation of new asset-holding entities;

(c) state and local government acquisition of sectoral assets which is financed by borrowing from the rest of the private sector;

(d) a higher level of credit sales to consumers.

No general and simple statement can be made about the amount of private indebtedness, since it is evident that a large variety of factors is relevant even if only the four examples just set out are considered. The forms of taxation can affect (a) and (b) in a variety of ways, for instance, while (b) presumably also depends partly upon the average size of firms. This in turn will reflect such variables as the size of the market and the proportion of the national income originating in agriculture. Thus the truisms just enunciated[1] cannot form the starting-point of a theoretical discussion but merely perform the service of indicating that private indebtedness is high when the savers are not those who invest.

Financial intermediaries must now be brought into the picture. They make possible the indirect holding of private

---

[1] I owe them to Dr Börje Kragh. See Ch. II of his *Prisbildningen på kreditmarknaden.*

debt and sectoral paper assets in the same way as non-financial corporations make possible the indirect ownership of real assets. Limited liability is a major factor which makes the latter attractive, and both types of indirect ownership may involve tax advantages. The shareholder in a business, for example, can have income turned into capital gains by the ploughing back of profits, while the depositor in a savings institution which holds mortgages may suffer less tax in total than if he held mortgages directly. None the less, tax considerations alone, can hardly explain the vast proliferation of financial intermediation, and some more fundamental factor must be invoked.

The problem can be put as follows. Financial intermediaries incur costs, so that the incomes paid out to the holders of their liabilities must be less, in total, than the income received from their assets. This means, then, that the holders of their liabilities receive less income than they would obtain if they held the assets directly. There must be some compensating advantages which induce them to do this. What are they?

The first advantage which springs to mind is that the intermediary supplies the service of breaking bulk. An individual with a small capital who wishes to spread it over a large number of assets can only do so at a prohibitive cost. This would not be the case if acquisition costs were always strictly proportional to the value of the asset and if all assets were highly divisible. These conditions are not fulfilled, however, for the very good reason that the paper work involved in, say, issuing one bond or paying a dividend, depends only to a small extent upon the issue price of the bond or the amount of the dividend.

There is a second advantage of indirect holding which also rests upon the provision of services by intermediaries. This is that the saver who does not know how to choose shares or to select mortgages delegates the choice to experts. It is of course possible for wealth owners to pay for advice without, so to speak, granting power of attorney and this is frequently done. The point is that to entrust one's principal to an intermediary is one way of obtaining a service which people are willing to pay for.

These are two advantages of indirect ownership. But are there not further advantages? The liabilities of intermediaries are surely something more than a mere pro-rating of their assets; there is some sort of transformation involved. Consider, for example, an investment trust with a fixed portfolio. If its only liability is its equity, the owner of one of its shares simply owns a fraction of its assets indirectly. The total income available to share-holders equals the total income accruing from its assets less the expenses of running the trust. This relationship is shown by the line JK in Diagram III, where total income is measured vertically and the income available to share-holders, 'net income', is measured horizontally. The expense of running the trust is OJ.

Now suppose that there are two classes of shares: preference shares and ordinary shares, between which the net income of the trust is divided. The part paid out to preference shareholders is given by the line JLM, while the rest of net income accrues to ordinary share-holders. Thus if total income in a particular year is OR, RS goes to preference shareholders and ST to ordinary shareholders. The investment trust has manufactured two types of asset which have different characteristics from an asset consisting simply of a fraction of its portfolio. Its two classes of shareholders have abandoned or delegated voting rights in the companies whose shares are held by the trust and they have sacrificed some income to meet the expense of running the trust. On the other hand they have had the services of experts and those of them whose shareholding is small have been able to diversify their

84

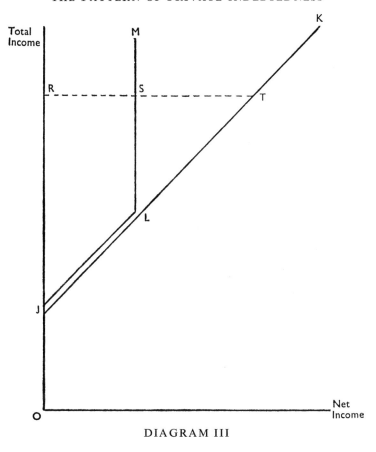

DIAGRAM III

assets to an extent otherwise impossible. In addition, with the creation of two classes of shares, the shareholders can now hold a lower or higher geared interest in the income from the portfolio than they could have done by direct ownership. Thus financial intermediation besides providing the services of breaking bulk and of expertize can

85

also provide investors with a different gearing (leverage) than they could obtain for themselves.

The establishment of the investment trust therefore enables the timorous and the pessimistic to obtain a safer first cut from total income than they could obtain by direct ownership. On the other hand the bold and the optimistic get a residual claim on a more uncertain share of total income than they could get by direct ownership. He who is little concerned by uncertainty or who views total income prospects in a rosy light is ready to concede to the fearful and gloomy a prior claim to a minimum which he expects to be exceeded. Both sorts of investor obtain an asset more tailored to their different requirements than direct ownership can offer and they are prepared to pay for this advantage by allowing the promoters of the investment trust to incur expenses and make some profit.

Where the ultimate borrower himself issues both debentures (bonds) and ordinary shares or preference shares and ordinary shares, those investors who are averse to uncertainty or who take an unfavourable view of profit prospects can obtain the sort of gearing they want without the assistance of any financial intermediary. They can buy only debentures or only ordinary shares or a combination of the two. The more largely that ordinary shares figure in their holding the higher the gearing of their interest in the company. What they cannot do by direct investment, however, is to obtain an interest which is more highly geared than the ordinary shares of the company; for this the interposition of the financial intermediary is required.

The conclusion of all this is that apart from breaking bulk and providing the service of management, financial intermediaries increase the range of gearing ratios between which wealth owners are free to choose. But this is not all, financial intermediaries manufacture liquidity and certainty as well as gearing.

Let us take as our example of the provision of liquidity a savings institution which invests in mortgages, holds a reserve of cash and whose major liability is savings deposits. It can for all practical purposes, guarantee withdrawal at short notice of these deposits while holding a cash reserve of only some few per cent. The reason is that the total of its deposits shows a far higher degree of stability than do many individual deposits. These individual deposits reflect the effects of a host of independent factors which frequently offset one another; the fluctuations in their total are consequently proportionally smaller. Thus the wealth owner who switches from direct ownership of mortgages to indirect ownership through deposits in the savings institution acquires far greater liquidity than he could have had himself by holding a cash reserve of the same percentage amount as that held by the institution, and the price he pays for this is limited to the part of the income from the mortgages which is required to defray the expenses of the institution.

There is another way in which liquidity is created. The breaking of bulk, already mentioned as a service rendered by intermediation, may not only enable the wealth owner to spread his risks. It may also reduce the minimum unit of investment or disinvestment. Thus a man cannot sell half of a mortgage, but he can withdraw half of a savings deposit; he cannot buy or sell £10 worth of Consuls but he can alter a deposit by £10. Hence, though breaking bulk may not in itself alter the liquidity of a man's total wealth, it does make it easier to turn a small part of that wealth into cash.

Just as savings institutions create liquidity in these two ways for their depositors as compared with direct investment in the same assets, so do life insurance companies

87

create certainty for their policy holders. The individual does not know when he is going to die, but his insurance company does know within limits when its policy holders in general are going to die so that it can supply him with the promise of a certain benefit even though this may turn out to be worth considerably more or considerably less than the accumulated value of his premiums.

The point that insurance involves the pooling of risks is too well known to require elaboration. What is important here is to note that life insurance companies and savings banks do the same thing; they supply to the individual the statistical properties of large aggregates, they sell the law of large numbers, enabling individuals to obtain as liquid an asset holding and as certain a prospect as is available to the public at large.

So much for the determinants of private indebtedness, which may be briefly summed up as lack of congruence between wealth and sectoral asset holding and the provision by intermediaries of more diversified, liquid and certain claims than would otherwise be available. The relation between this private indebtedness and the asset demands of the private sector regarded as a unit has already been discussed in Chapter V. It was shown there that shifts in demand away from private indebtedness towards a sectoral asset will raise the price of that sectoral asset relative to the other sectoral assets while shifts in demand from one sort of private debt to another will have little effect upon sectoral asset prices, that is, in the simple model, upon bond and real asset prices. It was also shown that the demand functions for sectoral assets so to speak include the effects of interaction between sectoral asset prices and the prices of private debt. We can now go a little farther in examining how private indebtedness affects the demand functions for sectoral assets.

One major facet of this problem has been the subject

of a good deal of discussion recently, namely the effects of the creation of liquid assets by financial intermediaries upon the demand for money. The Radcliffe report in England and the writings of Professors Gurley and Shaw in America have both suggested that some forms of private debt (i.e. intra-private-sector assets and liabilities) are important substitutes for money. If we express the matter in terms of income velocity we can say that the existence of the complex of financial intermediaries makes velocity greater than it would otherwise be and that it diminishes the changes in bond and real asset yields associated with changes in income velocity. The same thing can alternatively be stated in terms of the demand for money equation of Chapter IV:

$$D_M = aW + bH + kQ + jY$$

The existence of intermediaries makes some of these co-efficients lower than they otherwise would be, so that the demand for money is lowered. This is the first point. In addition, the existence of intermediaries makes j lower than it otherwise would be, so that an increase in income raises the demand for money by a smaller amount.

Both points are quite consistent with the present analysis. They follow from the proposition that financial intermediaries create liquidity and that they will expand the scale of their operations in response to an increased demand for liquidity. Wealth owners are induced to part with money in exchange for the liabilities of intermediaries which pass on the money to spenders by lending to them. Thus intermediaries facilitate an increase in the velocity of circulation of money by providing an increased volume of money substitutes.

The relevance of all this in the present context is that financial intermediaries shift the demand functions for net sectoral assets. The average yield on Federal obligations

89

therefore differs from what it would be if financial intermediaries were less developed. The recognition of the
importance of these institutions together with the distribution of wealth owners' asset preferences as determinants
of asset demands does not invalidate the argument of this
book, however. Provided that the functions show some
stability in the short run, the propositions of the theory
are useful. Over long periods one would expect the development of financial intermediaries to be numbered among
the factors responsible for gradual shifts in the functions.
While an analysis which brought financial intermediaries
explicitly into the analysis would no doubt add to the
theory, it would make it very complicated compared with
the simple aggregative approach adopted here. Hence the
mere fact that financial intermediaries affect the determination of asset prices constitutes no criticism of this
theory. The purpose of the theory is to derive some interesting and useful propositions about the main forces
responsible for changes in interest rates. The fact that other
factors relevant to interest rates can be enumerated is in no
way a criticism of the theory.

In summary, this chapter and Chapter V have brought
out some ways in which the price formation of net sectoral
assets is linked with the prices and structure of private
debt, i.e. of intrasectoral assets and liabilities. We have
seen how these phenomena affect the asset demands of the
consolidated private sector without attempting to place
them in the central exposition of the theory by restating it
in terms of a less aggregative model. The propositions
of the simple aggregative theory are not overthrown, but
we have now added to our understanding, particularly
concerning the role of financial intermediaries.

VIII

LONG- AND SHORT-TERM RATES
OF INTEREST

So far the analysis has dealt with the average yield on Federal obligations, without mention of the structure of the rates composing that average. If we leave aside differences in the tax treatment of Federal obligations and if we consider only those which are marketable, the major respect in which Federal obligations differ from one another is in their maturity. It is therefore the object of this chapter to examine the determinants of the maturity structure of interest rates on Federal obligations.

The literature on the structure of interest rates[1] contains at least three simple hypotheses concerning the way in which an individual wealth owner chooses between assets which differ only in respect of maturity. They are:

(1) each wealth owner knows with certainty the date at which he will need to realize his assets and endeavours to maximize the amount to which they will accumulate by that date. Thus his choice of Federal obligations depends upon current interest rates and his expectations concerning future interest

[1] See in particular Lutz, 'The Structure of Interest Rates', *Quarterly Journal of Economics*, November 1940 (reprinted in *Readings in the Theory of Income Distribution*); Culbertson, 'The Term Structure of Interest Rates', *Q.J.E.*, November 1957; Wehrle, 'Culbertson on Rate Structure', *Q.J.E.*, November 1958; Culbertson's reply, ibid., and Luckett, 'Professor Lutz and the Structure of Interest Rates', *Q.J.E.*, February 1959. This chapter builds heavily on Culbertson's paper and on unpublished discussion papers by David Meiselman and John H. Kareken.

rates. This may be called the 'expectations' hypothesis;

(2) each wealth owner is uncertain when he will need to realize his assets and is averse to uncertainty so that he will only hold obligations which experience shows to be more unstable in price than the average if they provide a yield above average to compensate him for the extra uncertainty. Thus since long-term obligations fluctuate more in price than short-term obligations, the wealth owner will only hold the former if they have a larger yield. This may be called the 'liquidity' hypothesis;

(3) each wealth owner endeavours to match the maturity structure of his assets and liabilities as closely as possible so as to minimize the risk of capital loss. Thus a life insurance company will hold obligations of greater maturity than a savings bank. This may be called the 'hedging' hypothesis.

All three of these hypotheses have something to be said for them, so rather than squabble about their relative merits it seems best to see whether they cannot be amalgamated. The liquidity hypothesis seems to be the special case of the hedging hypothesis where liabilities either will or may mature soon. Since, however, wealth owners frequently know with a fair degree of certainty that some of their liabilities will not mature for some time, the more general hedging hypothesis is to be preferred. On the other hand one important element in the liquidity hypothesis is worth retaining and that is the suggestion that the wealth owner's asset demands do not have a zero price elasticity and that he is prepared to sacrifice some liquidity for a higher yield and vice versa. Then bringing in the expectations hypothesis as well reminds us that the yield which is relevant to choice may not be just the yield to maturity implicit in current market quotations but also expected yields at one or more times in the future.

Instead of setting out a formal model of the wealth-owner's choice of the maturity structure of his holdings of Federal obligations, it will suffice to cast the relevant factors discussed above into a more coherent form by listing their effects one by one on a *ceteris paribus* basis. We suppose, then, that any of the following influences occurring in isolation would cause a wealth owner to shift towards longer maturities:

(*a*) an expectation that interest rates are going to fall;

(*b*) an expectation that the prices of long-term securities will be more stable than hitherto;

(*c*) an increase in longer term liabilities relative to liabilities which mature soon or at no certain time;

(*d*) a rise in current long-term rates relative to short-term.

These same factors will operate on an aggregative plane for all wealth owners taken together, i.e. for the private sector; in addition demand shifts may result from a redistribution of wealth between wealth owners. So much for the demand side of the analysis at an aggregative level, without reference to the structure of private indebtedness.

On the supply side stands the stock of Federal obligations which is a net liability of the monetary sector, equal to that part of the national debt which is held outside Government agencies, the central bank and the commercial banks. In the present context we treat its amount and composition as given exogenously.

We can now list the factors which will affect the maturity structure of interest rates. Long-term rates will fall relatively to short-term for example, if:

(*a*) the expectations of a substantial body of wealth owners concerning future interest rates change

93

towards a fall from a rise, towards a larger fall than before or towards a smaller rise than before;

(*b*) a substantial body of wealth owners come to regard long-term Federal obligations as more stable in price than hitherto;

(*c*) wealth-owners' long-term liabilities rise in relation to total liabilities;

(*d*) the average maturity of Federal obligations falls.

These propositions have the merit that they are consistent with either an upward- or a downward-sloping curve relating yields to maturity. Although the curve has been downward-sloping (short-term rates in excess of long-term) only very rarely in the U.S. since the early thirties, it was too frequent a phenomenon in earlier periods for us to be able to regard it as an exceptional condition.

Whichever way the curve slopes, if it maintains its direction of slope and general level over an extended period we can hardly call in (*a*) above as an explanation of the direction of slope. If, for instance, short-term rates exceed long-term rates for a few years and we attribute this to a prevalent expectation that rates will decline, we are supposing that wealth owners fail to readjust their expectations when the decline fails to materialize, that they fail to learn from experience. Fortunately this difficult assumption is not forced upon us, for there are three much more plausible possible reasons for a downward-sloping curve, corresponding to (*b*), (*c*) and (*d*) above. Firstly, long-term obligations may be generally expected to show only small fluctuations in price, so that they are thought to offer a fairly stable capital value as well as a stable interest income. Secondly, wealth-owners' commitments and liabilities may be rather long term and, thirdly, the average maturity of the debt may be rather short.

The point that people endeavour to match the maturity pattern of assets and liabilities is illustrated by Diagram IV which relates to all U.S. corporations other than banks and insurance companies. The vertical axis shows the sum of retained profits, depreciation and long-term external sources of funds during the year, while the horizontal axis shows expenditure on plant and equipment as a percentage of total uses of funds during the year.[1] There is a positive correlation of ·96 between the two, indicating that long-term sources of finance are resorted to when long-term assets are acquired. This result is confirmed by cross-section data on the assets and liabilities of non-financial corporations contained in *Statistics of Income*.[2]

Treating the private sector as a unit means that the maturity distribution of net sectoral assets and liabilities other than Federal obligations is one of the determinants of the maturity pattern of the demand for Federal obligations. If these other assets are predominantly long term and the liabilities are short term, short-term Federal obligations will be heavily in demand. Conversely, the larger the private sector's holding of money in relation to its stock of real assets and the greater the fraction of private debt held by the monetary sector which is long term, the longer will be the average maturity of Federal obligations demanded.

The simplifying assumption which this aggregative treatment implies is that the maturity pattern of net sectoral assets and liabilities reflects the maturity pattern of the gross assets and liabilities of the holders of Federal

[1] Based on 'Sources and Use of Corporate Funds 1946–57', Table V–10 in *U.S. Income and Output* (U.S. Department of Commerce).

[2] Mr. David Meiselman found the ratios of short-term and long-term assets and liabilities of corporations in the 57 non-financial industrial categories to have a correlation coefficient of ·872 in the 1951 data. I am also indebted to him for suggesting the use of sources and uses of funds data in this context.

95

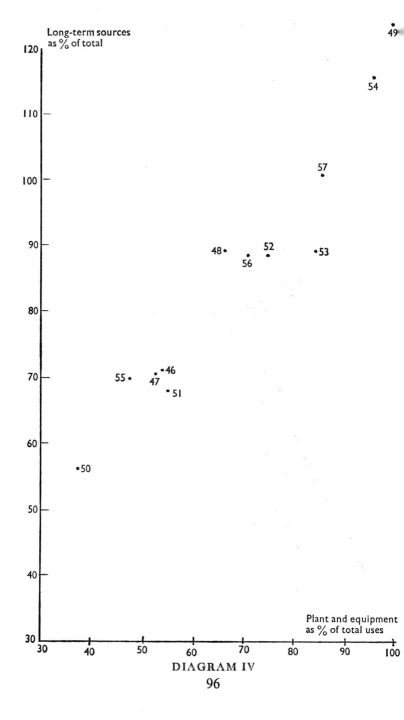

DIAGRAM IV

96

obligations. In other words it has to be assumed that the pattern of private indebtedness makes no difference to the demand of the private sector. Now there is at least one very good reason why this should not be the case in practice, namely the point made in the previous chapter that financial intermediaries create liabilities which have different characteristics from their assets. Savings institutions which hold Federal obligations among their assets and whose deposits are redeemable at short notice in effect shorten the maturity of the obligations they hold. Hence the effect of an increased average maturity of Federal obligations, in raising long-term rates relative to short-term rates will be cushioned by an expansion of financial intermediaries, assuming that short-term rates are below long-term rates. The creation or widening of a gap between the two promises higher profits to the intermediaries and enables them to raise the rate which they offer on deposits relative to the yields obtaining on short-term Federal obligations.

There is therefore at least one way in which the pattern of private indebtedness makes the maturity distribution of Federal obligations demanded by the private sector weaker at the short end than one would infer from the maturity distribution of other net sectoral assets and liabilities. None the less, though this mechanism may cushion the impact of forces working to effect changes in the maturity structure of interest rates, it is unlikely to reverse them. Thus in the run of a few years or so, in periods during which there are no major shifts in the distribution of wealth and no important financial innovations, the crudities involved in aggregation are probably not so strong as to vitiate the influence of the four factors (a), (b), (c) and (d) listed above as causing changes in the relationship between short-term and long-term rates.

A proper test of the theory advanced would require an attempt to measure:

97

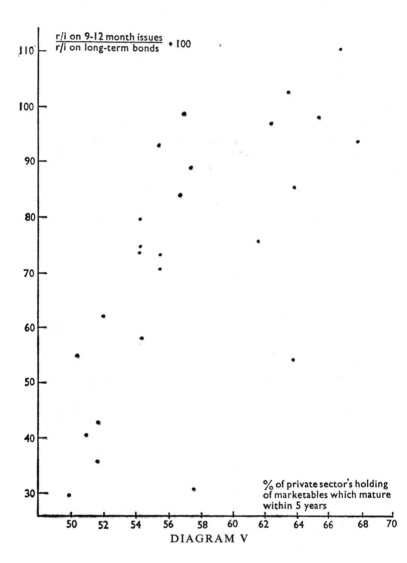

DIAGRAM V

(a) changes in expectations concerning future rates;
(b) changes in attitude concerning the general stability of the prices of long-term Federal obligations;
(c) changes in the maturity structure of the other sectoral assets and the sectoral liabilities of the private sector;
(d) changes in the maturity structure of the stock of Federal obligations held by the private sector.

Only the fourth of these is at all simple. The U.S. Treasury survey of the ownership of the public debt makes it possible to calculate the percentage of interest-bearing public marketable securities held by the private sector which mature within five years.[1] The higher this percentage is, the lower is the average length of Federal obligations on a first approximation. A rough measure of the interest-rate structure is provided by expressing the average rate of interest on 9–12-month U.S. Government securities as a percentage of the yield on U.S. long-term bonds.[2]

The two percentages just described are plotted quarterly for the years 1953–8 inclusive in Diagram V. They show a positive correlation of ·65, which is in accordance with theoretical expectation. No seasonality is apparent. It is thus clear that changes on the supply side were a major determinant of changes in the maturity pattern of interest rates on Federal obligations during the fifties as suggested above.

This is not an adequate test, but it does suggest that the approach of this book can usefully be applied to an examination of the structure as well as the level of interest rates on Federal obligations.

[1] The data are taken from the table 'Ownership of U.S. Government marketable and convertible securities' which appears regularly in the *Federal Reserve Bulletin*. The figures relate to the end of the month.

[2] These rates appear in the tables 'Money Market Rates' and 'Bond and Stock Yields' in the *Federal Reserve Bulletin*. For most of the period the 'old series' of the long-term rate was used. The rates are both *monthly* averages of daily figures.

IX

FURTHER DEVELOPMENTS

THERE are several directions in which the approach of
this book could usefully be extended. In the preceding
chapter a start was made at analysing the maturity structure of interest rates on Federal obligations. We shall now
conclude by presenting a preliminary discussion of two
other problems, suggesting how the first should be approached and how the second should not be approached.

The first of these is the problem of bringing the behaviour of the commercial banking system into the
analysis. So far the commercial banks have been lumped
together with the monetary authorities and their actions
treated as exogenous. It is clear, however, that the commercial banking system behaves rather differently from
the monetary authorities. Commercial banks are run in
order to earn profits and consequently their behaviour
ought to be susceptible of economic analysis. Hence there
is a case for separating them from the monetary authori-
ities, i.e. from the central bank and Government. The
picture of the monetary system which results from this
separation is shown in Table VII.

The asset classification is rather more complicated than
that of Chapter VI since liquid assets have been split into
four items: money which is the liability of the monetary
authorities, bank deposits, savings bonds and, a negative
item, bank loans. The first of these, sometimes called
'high-powered money', provides the private sector with its
currency and banks with their cash base. The second item
is a liability of the banks, the third is held by banks only

FURTHER DEVELOPMENTS

TABLE VII

	Monetary Authorities	Commercial Banks	Private Sector
Currency and Federal Reserve Deposits	L	A	A
Demand and Time Deposits	—	L	A
Savings Bonds	L	*	A
Bank Loans	—	A	L
Federal Obligations	L	A	A
Long-term Debt	A	A	L

to an insignificant extent and the fourth is a liability of the private sector only.

If a model is to be made of asset price formation in terms of the three sectors here distinguished, the model of earlier chapters must be changed in three ways. Firstly, the single demand function of the private sector for liquid assets must be replaced by separate functions for each of the four items listed above. Secondly, the exogenous variables other than income and real assets must now relate exclusively to the behaviour of the monetary authorities. The list of independent variables therefore becomes the following:[1]

- (a) the amount of currency and member bank deposits at the Federal Reserve System plus the amount of savings bonds outstanding;
- (b) the quantity of Federal obligations outstanding, now including those held by commercial banks;
- (c) the amount of long-term debt held by the monetary authorities;
- (d) the interest rate paid on saving bonds;

[1] Three minor factors are disregarded here, namely postal savings deposits, Federal deposits at commercial banks, and the fact that commercial banks hold a (very small) amount of savings bonds.

101

(*e*) the quantity of real assets;
(*f*) the level of national income.

There is a corresponding change in the list of dependent variables, the most important alteration being that the quantity of commercial bank deposits now enters this list. Interest rates on bank loans also become an endogenous variable.

Before anything can be done with this new model, its construction requires a third innovation to be introduced into the earlier two-sector model: behaviour equations are now needed for the commercial banking sector. The banks are shown as having four assets in Table VII and one liability, deposits (their equity being omitted). What factors determine the total of their deposits, the rate they offer on time deposits, their loan charges and the composition of their assets?

In view of the fact that the United States contains more banking statistics than any other country, one might expect a good deal of quantitative information to be available about the behaviour of banks. Unfortunately, this is not the case, and the literature on the aggregative economics of banking does not go far beyond the discussion of a few simple ratios. If:

m = the ratio maintained by the private sector between currency on the one hand and commercial bank deposits on the other;
e = the ratio maintained by commercial banks between currency and Federal Reserve deposits on the one hand and their own deposits on the other;

then commercial bank deposits will be $\dfrac{1}{c+m}$ of the total

amount of currency and Federal Reserve deposits not held

inside the monetary authority sector. Now m relates to the behaviour of the private sector, not the banks,[1] and we know that c is partly determined by the composition of deposits in relation to the complexities of the reserve requirements imposed upon banks which are members of the Federal Reserve System. But little has been written about the other factors which determine c or about the factors which determine the composition of the other assets of commercial banks. Professor A. J. Brown's admirable and pioneering econometric study of the behaviour of the London clearing banks,[2] has had no imitators. While it has been shown that American bankers alter the total of their earnings assets fairly promptly in response to changes in their reserves adjusted to allow for the complexities resulting from reserve requirements, and that during 1953–5 c was lower when interest rates were rising than when they were falling,[3] that is about all—in print, at least.

All we can do here, therefore, is to assume that the different assets held by banks are substitutes for one another to a greater or less extent. Since current yield is one, though only one, of the characteristics of assets which determines their attractiveness to bankers, it follows that *ceteris paribus* a fall in the current yield on any one asset will cause some shift away from it towards other assets. Professor Brown's paper supports this proposition in the case of the London clearing banks in the inter-war period.

This proposition is insufficient, when linked with the

[1] Philip Cagan has made an important contribution concerning m. See his paper, 'The demand for currency relative to the total money supply', *Journal of Political Economy*, August 1958.

[2] 'The Liquidity Preference Schedules of the London Clearing Banks', *Oxford Economic Papers*, No. 1, 1938.

[3] See George Horwich, 'Elements of timing and response in the balance sheet of banking, 1953–55', *Journal of Finance*, May, 1957.

rest of the model, to provide an analysis of the determination of the volume of bank deposits, the interest rate on bank loans or the division of the stock of Federal obligations outstanding between the private sector and the commercial bank sector. If, however, we add to it the assumption that bank assets are all superior with respect to bank resources, something can be said about the determination of the average interest rate on Federal obligations.

Consider the first of the set of exogenous variables listed above, the amount of currency, Federal Reserve deposits and savings bonds outstanding. The composition of this total can be changed at will by the private sector and banks since these three items are convertible into one another. Suppose that the amount increases, the other exogenous variables being unaltered and the behaviour functions of the commercial banks and private sector remaining unchanged. If the increase accrues to the private sector, it will seek to distribute the increment in wealth between all assets and will thus pull up asset prices. If it accrues to the banks, they will buy Federal obligations and long-term debt from the private sector, thus reducing its holdings of these assets and increasing its money holding. The banks may also increase the availability and lower the cost of bank loans. All these changes will, as we saw in Chapter VI, tend to lower interest rates on Federal obligations. Thus in either case the end result of the assumed increment in the liquid liabilities of the monetary authorities will be a fall in the average interest rate on Federal obligations.

Suppose instead that the second exogenous variable, the amount of Federal obligations outstanding, is increased. This will raise their average interest rate. Note that it may also lead to some increase in the quantity of bank deposits, since a rise in interest rates may cause the banks to lower

104

c and the private sector to lower m (particularly if the banks raise the interest paid on time deposits).

The way in which these exogenous changes are made will naturally affect the course of events. But given the *ceteris paribus* assumption, the nature of the impact upon the equilibrium level of interest rates on Federal obligations is unambiguous, and since the analysis is static it is only the characteristic of alternative equilibrium positions with which we are concerned. Thus if the monetary authorities create more Federal Reserve deposits and acquire more long-term debt, it makes no difference, at the present level of aggregation, whether they acquire it from the banks or from the private sector. In either case the new equilibrium position will differ from the old one in that, *inter alia*, interest rates on Federal obligations will be lower.

All this suffices to show that the propositions developed earlier all hold good, with appropriate reformulation, when the commercial banks are brought into the picture. A full analysis would require a great deal more information, would be very complicated and would explain a wider range of phenomena. It is to be hoped that American economists will devote some attention to the subject.

Let us now turn to a second extension of the theory, namely analysis of the determination of share (stock) prices. It was shown in Chapter V how share prices and the prices of Federal obligations are linked. While shares and Federal obligations are substitutes for individual wealth owners they are not so for the private sector as a whole. Consequently the stock of shares in existence is not an independent variable of the theory in the same way as the stock of Federal obligations.

If shares and share prices are to be brought into the picture explicitly, shares must be made an intersector item. This means that the private sector must be split into

105

two sectors one of which owns shares and the other of which—corporations—issues shares. Consistency then requires that all the assets and liabilities of these sectors also be brought into the analysis. The non-corporate private sector holds fixed-interest corporate securities as well as shares and has liabilities to the corporate sector in the shape of consumer credit. The minimum number of variables which would have to enter into the analysis would therefore include at least all the items in Table VIII.

TABLE VIII

	Monetary Sector	Corporate Sector	Non-corporate Private Sector
Money and Savings Bonds less Bank Loans	L	A	A
Federal Obligations	L	A	A
Corporate Bonds	—	L	A
Shares	—	L	A
Other Long-term Debt	A	L	L
Trade Credit	—	A	L
Real Assets	—	A	A

If a model is constructed in terms of these variables it will explain not only the price of shares but also the prices and yields of corporate bonds, Federal obligations and real assets. In order to construct it, asset demand and supply functions will be needed for both of the two private sectors. The demand for each asset and supply of each liability presumably depends *inter alia* on wealth, income and the yield of all assets and liabilities. Since the budget constraint enables us to leave one asset demand function of each sector implicit and since we can treat the behaviour of the monetary sector as exogenous we are therefore left with the requirement of setting out twelve asset demand-supply functions, most of them with up to nine terms. Thus if simple linear functions are assumed in the same way as in Chapters II and IV there will be up to 108 coefficients.

Even if some of the coefficients are assumed to be zero it is apparent that the algebraic solution would be too complicated to be interesting. The problem cannot therefore be approached in this way without some drastic simplifications.

This is not a satisfactory conclusion, but it is as far as I can take the matter. The essential point is that the analysis must be extremely complex because it has to be less aggregative than in the case of net sectoral assets.

This ends the book. But I do not pretend that the analysis is finished. Clearly there is a lot to be done and I hope that others will be persuaded to carry on with the work. I have endeavoured to set out a simple model which is suitable for incorporation in textbooks. The approach followed is a simple and common-sense one whose relevance to the real world is direct and obvious. I have shown how it can be applied and tested and have pointed out some of the directions in which it might be developed. The analysis has not built 'irrefutable theorems into an empty edifice of compounded tautologies' but has employed 'questionable premises . . . to obtain questionable conclusions'[1] which seems to me the right way to approach economic phenomena.

[1] Cf. page 1 of Professor Baumol's *Business Behaviour, Value and Growth*.

INDEX

108

GEORGE ALLEN & UNWIN LTD
London: 40 *Museum Street, W.C.*1

Auckland: 24 *Wyndham Street*
Sydney, N.S.W.: Bradbury House, 55 *York Street*
Cape Town: 109 *Long Street*
Bombay: 15 *Graham Road, Ballard Estate, Bombay* 1
Calcutta: 17 *Chittaranjan Avenue, Calcutta* 13
New Delhi: 13-14 *Ajmeri Gate Extension, New Delhi* 1
Karachi: Meherson's Estate, Wood Street, Karachi 2
Mexico: Villalongin 32-10, *Piso, Mexico* 5, *D.F.*
Toronto: 91 *Wellington Street West*
São Paulo: Avenida 9 *de Julho* 1138-*Ap.* 51
Buenos Aires: Escritorio 454-459, *Florida* 165
Singapore: 36c *Princep Street, Singapore* 7
Hong Kong: 1/12 *Mirador Mansions, Kowloon*

MONEY, CREDIT, NATIONAL INCOME AND EMPLOYMENT

ERICH SCHNEIDER   *Demy 8vo. About 28s. net*

This famous text-book falls into two parts. The first deals with the theory of money creation and destruction. The author illustrates the essential principles by considering various models of banking systems.

The second part gives a systematic, detailed and rigorous account of the modern theory of income and employment determination. The author builds up the theory gradually from the simplest to more complicated models. Thus, for example, the student is taken from the model of 'a closed economy without a government' to one in which government expenditure and revenue affect the level of national income, and to one in which exports, imports and rates of exchange help to determine income and employment; from a model in which the rate of interest and quantity of money have no effects to one in which they are variables relevant to the determination of income; and from a model in which capital stock is assumed constant to one in which it is growing. The author examines both the static and dynamic properties of most of the models.

INDIAN ECONOMIC POLICY AND DEVELOPMENT

P. T. BAUER   *Demy 8vo. About 16s. net*

In this important new book Mr Bauer reviews the major elements of official Indian development policy, considers their economic implications and their probable political and economic results. He then examines alternative approaches to the promotion of development. The development plans, notably the Second Five Year Plan and the official outlines of the Third Plan, receive major attention, but the author also considers other official policies and measures affecting economic development, which do not usually figure prominently in the formal development plans. He reviews the Indian economic and social scene, since without an understanding of this background it is impossible to assess the merits of alternative policies and methods.

Mr Bauer considers specific themes, including the influence of social customs and attitudes on economic progress; the relationship between investment expenditure and economic development; inter-relationships between agriculture and industry; and the importance of certain major political objectives.

THE USE OF ECONOMIC STATISTICS

C. A. BLYTH *In preparation. Demy 8vo. 28s. net, cloth; 22s. net, paper*

This is an elementary introduction to the sources of economic statistics and their uses in answering economic questions.

The author's approach is novel in that he introduces statistical methods as tools to be used in examining economic problems. Each chapter deals with a typical problem of applied economics and explains in detail the statistical sources and methods required. Emphasis is placed upon the framing of hypotheses, the selection of appropriate statistics and the testing of the hypotheses by inspection. The economic problems—such as the present position of the cotton industry; the effect of hire purchase controls upon car sales; the extent to which prices have risen since the war, etc.—are so chosen and arranged that statistical subjects are presented to the student in an understandable way. The statistical subjects covered in this manner include the standard British sources, tabular and graphical presentation, index numbers of prices, distributions and their characteristics, the social accounts and real income, American and European statistics, and the measurement of economic relationships by scatter diagrams. Each chapter contains exercises with hints as to their solution.

CASES AND PROBLEMS IN ECONOMICS

PROFESSOR JAMES S. DUESENBERRY and
PROFESSOR L. E. PRESTON *In preparation. Demy 8vo. 15s. net*

The teaching of economics on the basis of real-life problems is gaining ground, but we are still indebted to America for adequate source material. The two experienced authors have provided 'a large stock of excellent problems . . . culled from real life which will be a great boon to us'—to quote from our adviser's report—'and a very important and welcome contribution to the material available for teaching economics in this country'.

It seems likely that there will be a big demand for the book and its price should make it possible for each student to have his own copy. The cases selected call for the application of economic analysis to the problems of the firm, of the market and of the economy as a whole. In each case the student is obliged to demonstrate his grasp of theory against a thoroughly practical background in which it will quickly be apparent whether the solution makes sense. This collection can be used from the first year onwards and all but the simplest problems can be handled at various levels of sophistication, which gives it great flexibility in the hands of the teacher.

GEORGE ALLEN & UNWIN LTD